I0518397

OUTRAGEOUS

THE WORDS OF JESUS THAT TURN OUR WORLD UPSIDE DOWN

RADIANT STUDY SERIES

EDITED BY

AUTUMN RICHARDSON

JEANNE FOUST

MELISSA MCFERRIN

CYPRESS

Copyright © 2025

Manufactured in the United States of America

Cataloging-in-Publication Data

Outrageous: the words of Jesus that turn our world upside down. Radiant study series/ edited by Autumn Richardson, Jeanne Foust, Melissa McFerrin.

p. cm.

ISBN 979-8-89733-013-3 (pbk.) 979-8-89733-014-0 (ebook)

Library of Congress Control Number: 2025944265

1. Bible—Study and teaching. 2. Sermon on the Mount—Study and teaching. 3. Christian life—Study and teaching. I. Richardson, Autumn, editor. II. Foust, Jeanne, editor. III. McFerrin, Melissa, editor. IV. Title. V. Series.

226.9060071—dc20

Cover design by Abby Foust.

Cypress Publications
3625 Helton Drive
PO Box HCU
Florence, AL 35630

www.hcu.edu

CONTENTS

INTRODUCTION

JEANNE FOUST

Preposterous. Radical. Unexpected. Revolutionary. Outrageous. Choosing a title for this book turned out to be one of the biggest challenges of the whole process. *How can we describe Jesus' teachings in a word? How can we capture the way He turned the Jews' understanding of scripture and godly living on its head? How can we be transformed by His words and life to love people more like He did? How do we live well in this upside-down kingdom He preached?*

His words were more than theoretical; they provided practical but unconventional instructions about turning the other cheek, going the second mile, loving our enemies, and storing up treasures in heaven. He talked about hard things like forgiving and denying ourselves and not worrying, and he flipped human nature's "me first" attitude to look, well, more like Him—humble, serving, loving. It was, and still is, an outrageous way to live.

Jesus knew His teachings would be difficult for many to reconcile. He knew His love was radical. He not only talked about sacrificial living, but He demonstrated it in the most selfless of ways...preposterous, revolutionary love on a cross.

Outrageous even! The Apostle Paul called it nonsense for some: "For the message of the cross is foolishness to those who are perishing, but to us who are being saved it is the power of God" (1 Corinthians 1:18 NIV), but not for us. For Christians, it is the "power of God" to live in ways that might look outrageous to the world.

There's also something else that might be *unexpected* about this book. All eight authors are younger than thirty years old. Embracing 1 Timothy 4:12, these young women speak truth and wisdom and love through their writing. With spiritual depth and biblical insight, they share their perspectives about countercultural living in ways that are both personal and inspiring.

Whether you use *Outrageous* for personal or group Bible study, we pray you learn, grow, and think about what it means to be revolutionary followers of Jesus! Enjoy the bonus material throughout; we hope you will be blessed and find something preposterous about Him and the abundant life He has promised His people!

"Tough Love"
Ava Johnson

> *Tough love is effective or so I am told.*
> *A tactic used since the days of old*
> *Expectations set, tenderness I withhold*
> *Until you reflect my wishes and you obey my scold*
>
> *Tough love is my way to keep you in check*
> *For you to stay in bounds so your life's not a wreck*
> *Live up to my standards with your shortened hand from*
> *   the deck*
> *I see past my log to judge your speck.*

But what if tough love isn't what I have made it?
Is tough love the love that my God created?
Is this the love that flows down when my spirit is faded
Or is true tough love something Christ adumbrated

Maybe true tough love is loving when it's tough
When others are hateful and their edges are rough
When cards are on the table and intention calls your
 bluff
When they betray, slander, and exploit, is love really
 enough?

Jesus' tough love is constant in the valley and peak
He put down his stone and turned the other cheek
He laid up in heaven the treasure we seek
He walked a second mile in the shoes of the meek

He didn't worry about tomorrow or what others think
Forgave infinitely, despite the bitter cup to drink
He's perfect and saves us when we sink
Follow with my cross, and my ego shrink.

Tough love is helping others reach their crown
By helping them out of the mud, not pushing them
 further down
Not judging with disgust, face holding a frown
By love we can turn the world upside down.

Love is patient, kind, and contagious
To change the world we must first change us
By imitating the path the Most High paved us
Jesus' kind of tough love is outrageous.

SONGS FOR THE JOURNEY

As you make your way through the *Outrageous* teachings of Jesus in this book, the Radiant team has put together a *Spotify* playlist to help you sit with the message a bit longer. These hymns echo the themes of Kingdom living found in each chapter. Whether you listen quietly, sing along in the car, or share in worship with your study group, we hope these songs help you carry Jesus's words with you.

Search **Spotify** for Radiant-OUTRAGEOUS to access the playlist:
https://open.spotify.com/playlist/4kyYdtfrs1ppv70SS banlE?si=4Hg6oT-JTaeIGFUmXgFIQA

CHAPTER 1
TURN THE OTHER CHEEK

MATTHEW 5:39; LUKE 6:29

TRISTIN WOOD

STEPPING INTO THE CHALLENGE

EVERY NIGHT, as I put my two-year-old daughter to bed, my husband starts a movie. By the time I've brushed her teeth, listened to her prayer, helped her pick the perfect stuffies, and finally tucked her in, the movie is already twenty to thirty minutes in. And every night, I have a secret scavenger hunt on my phone to figure out the name of the movie he's watching just based on the actors, setting, and events. Then, I read the plot synopsis to catch up if it looks like something I care to watch.

At first, this annoyed me. He couldn't wait until I got back? But over time, I actually started to *enjoy* looking up his movies. I realized that I love learning how movies are made; I find a behind-the-scenes look at props, sound design, food styling, and animation endlessly fascinating.

Even the screenwriting process holds captivating secrets. In writing a film, screenwriters often use "tropes," or repeated themes and motifs across a genre. Although it appears in many other films, a trope known as *"Well, THAT just happened"* is especially associated with the Marvel Cinematic Universe. When characters start to get too emotional or a moment feels too serious, the scene suddenly whips to a sarcastic tone to lighten the mood, often reducing any real emotion to a goofy joke. This trope isn't exclusive to Marvel movies; in fact, it's been around much longer than you might expect. *Bathos*, as defined by Britannica, refers to a sudden, unexpected shift from serious to trivial, often for comedic effect. The term was first used in 1728.[1]

Tropes in film often reflect the deeper values of the culture they come from. For millennia, people have believed that repressing vulnerability is a valid way to defend oneself from pain or humiliation. This shows up in the behavior of many popular movie characters. We have been trained to believe that sensitivity is weak and embarrassing. Unfortunately, when a person is inevitably hurt and they see that their hardened exterior hasn't protected them, they tend to lash out toward others in response. Movies are only a fantasy, but emotional suppression and retaliation are very real, and they can cause real harm.

GOING DEEPER

It didn't take long after the creation of men for them to show vengeful behavior. In Genesis 4:3–8, Cain's jealousy and anger led to the murder of his brother. Only two chapters later, Genesis 6:11–13 says men were so violent toward each other that God wiped them off the Earth with the flood. Then Joseph's brothers tried to kill him because they were jealous of him in Genesis 37.

God saw that humankind was struggling with extreme retaliation, so He put some regulations in place. In the Old Testament, God iterated and reiterated the law of retaliation, called "*lex talionis*," as demonstrated in these verses:

- "But if there is harm, then you shall pay life for life, eye for eye, tooth for tooth, hand for hand, foot for foot, burn for burn, wound for wound, stripe for stripe" (Exod 21:23–25 ESV).

- "Fracture for fracture, eye for eye, tooth for tooth; whatever injury he has given a person shall be given to him" (Lev 24:20).
- "Your eye shall not pity. It shall be life for life, eye for eye, tooth for tooth, hand for hand, foot for foot" (Deut 19:21).

These passages sound harsh, but *lex talionis* was not intended to *encourage* retaliation, but rather to *discourage* it. *Lex talionis* was established as a form of justice to prevent offenders from receiving greater punishment than they deserved.[2]

Unfortunately, humanity has a way of twisting God's words. Instead of using this law as a form of justice, the Jews were taking it as an excuse to "get back" at their wrongdoers. In Jesus's day, this delight in retaliation still continued, so He admonished the people to look at their hearts:

- "But I say to you who hear, Love your enemies, do good to those who hate you, bless those who curse you, pray for those who abuse you. To one who strikes you on the cheek, offer the other also, and from one who takes away your cloak do not withhold your tunic either. Give to everyone who begs from you, and from one who takes away your goods do not demand them back. And as you wish that others would do to you, do so to them" (Luke 6:27–31).
- "You have heard that it was said, 'Eye for eye, and tooth for tooth.' But I tell you, do not resist an evil person. If anyone slaps you on the right cheek, turn to them the other cheek also. And if anyone wants to sue you and take your shirt, hand over your coat as well. If anyone forces you to go one mile, go with them two miles. Give to the one who asks you, and do not turn away from the one who wants to borrow from you" (Matt 5:38–42 NIV).

Just like the Israelites and the Jews of Jesus's day, people *still* resort to retaliation and aggression when they feel they have been wronged: Clapping back. Subtweeting. Karens. Petty. Drama. Roasting. Feuds. Diss tracks. Throwing shade. Exposing. Canceling. Dragging. Doxxing. These are all modern terms that relate to one concept: revenge.

Without even realizing it, we absorb this information about expected behavior and integrate it into our lives. We think we have to protect ourselves to survive. So when all the social media posts, jokes, and movies are gone and real life hits, we really do lash out at others who harm us as a form of protection, and it's not usually funny like it is online. In those moments, it feels serious because when we are acting defensively, it is because we are hurting or emotionally drained. Personally, I struggle to remain kind when I am stressed, but it has never made me feel better when I snap at someone.

Jesus knows this, of course, and teaches us a better way. Simply put, "turning the other cheek" means that we are not to retaliate against an aggressor. It means that we show kindness instead, relieving us of the duty of judgment and putting any due punishment in the hands of God, the only perfect judge.

Repay no one evil for evil, but give thought to do what is honorable in the sight of all. If possible, so far as it depends on you, live peaceably with all. Beloved, never avenge yourselves, but leave it to the wrath of God, for it is written, "Vengeance is mine, I will repay, says the Lord." To the contrary, "if your enemy is hungry, feed him; if he is thirsty, give him something to drink; for by so doing you will heap burning coals on his head." Do not be overcome by evil, but overcome evil with good. (Rom 12:17–21 ESV)

Jesus was the ultimate example of how to conduct ourselves in conflict. Many times throughout the Gospels, He was confronted by Jewish leaders seeking to make Him look foolish or blasphemous. Not once did He retaliate to protect Himself (1 Pet 2:23). Jesus went through a mockery of a trial and did not defend Himself (Matt 27:13–14). When He was tortured on the cross, not only did He go peacefully (Isa 53:7), but He actually prayed for His tormentors (Luke 23:34).

This is an incredibly difficult teaching; it goes directly against our innate human desire for self-preservation. For that reason, it is common to misunderstand Jesus's teaching or be resistant to it. To better understand this teaching, we should take a holistic, balanced look at Scripture. We need to weigh each passage against other passages.

When someone wrongs us, it is very easy to pout or play the victim. This is a symptom of changing our actions, but not changing our heart. The Pharisees were very good at doing things to be seen by others, and Jesus rebuked them for it (Matt 6:1–6; 23:2–36; John 12:42–43).

Sadly, many people believe that turning the other cheek is allowing others to do as they please with no recourse. This is inaccurate as well. We are not meant to be pitiful doormats, constantly suffering in sadness. Yes, Jesus did promise that there would be conflict in this life (Matt 10:34–36), but He also promised that we would enjoy a fulfilling, spiritually abundant life (John 10:10). How can that be?

LIVING IT OUT

Pain in life is inevitable. Although we cannot avoid all conflict, we do control how we handle the inevitable strife of life. It all starts in the heart. If we simply change our actions without changing the way we are thinking, we will end up as the victim or the doormat.

I have spent many unfortunate years struggling to turn the other cheek. Here are some strategies that have helped me on my journey.

Abide in God

As a special education teacher, I often work with children who struggle in social situations. Sometimes, we will use a tool called "social stories." The idea is that a child cannot learn while in crisis mode, so we teach proper ways to handle stressors long before they arise. We repeatedly practice proper coping techniques so that when the student encounters an upsetting event in real life, the appropriate response is second nature. Similarly, as Christians, we must learn and practice before our ability to turn the other cheek is tested (Prov 4:23).

The first strategy is drawing on the love that comes from abiding in God. We cannot share love with others if we are empty ourselves or afraid that someone will hurt our hearts. However, there is no need to lash out to protect ourselves from people if there is plenty of love to share instead (Eph 2:4–5; Rom 5:6–8; 1 John 4:7–12). God's love is strong enough to carry us through anything and is impervious to all the things we throw at Him (Rom 8:38–39). Even if we have just a sliver of that love inside of us, we will be stronger. If we feel love and compassion for others, it will be harder for them to hurt us.[3] We know that there is nothing man can do to us. I can attest to the fact that when my relationship with God is stronger, my relationships with others are also stronger.

We grow our relationship with God, just as we would with a friend, by spending time with Him. We talk to Him in prayer and listen to Him through His word. As an example of this growth in my life, I used to pray for God to "help me know what to say to people," and it worked (Jas 1:5). The more time we spend with God, the stronger a foundation we will have in Him.

> Everyone then who hears these words of mine and does them will be like a wise man who built his house on the rock. And the rain fell, and the floods came, and the winds blew and beat on that house, but it did not fall, because it had been founded on

the rock. And everyone who hears these words of mine and does not do them will be like a foolish man who built his house on the sand. And the rain fell, and the floods came, and the winds blew and beat against that house, and it fell, and great was the fall of it. (Matt 7:24–27)

Someone who uses their own defenses may have their own moats and cannons, but they are still built on the sand. Their defenses will do no good against a storm, and they will still fall. Jesus is the only way we can be safe in life's storms and know how to respond to others in a loving, godly way.

Remove the Focus from Your Own Pain

Sometimes people harm others because of a simple accident or misunderstanding. Hanlon's Razor states:

> "Never attribute to malice that which can be adequately explained by neglect, ignorance or incompetence." … When we are slighted or ignored, it's all too easy to assume malicious intent, all the while forgetting how many times we have treated others in a similar way. In reality, people are as neglectful, distracted, tired, misunderstanding, and incompetent as us. It is rarely the case that they are malicious.[4]

Some people do hurt others on purpose because they have their own pain. My dad always says, "Hurt people hurt people." When confronted with conflict, try getting curious about why others are acting in such a way. Understanding will help us to practice compassion. Ask yourself, "Are they okay?" Remind yourself that the situation may not really be about you. You would never see someone who was crying and walk up to them to kick dirt in their eye! So, if we recognize that someone is hurting, let's try to approach the situation with concern rather than contempt.

When someone hurts us, and they see that we aren't playing the game, they may wonder why. This is a perfect opportunity to show them the peace that God's love can give. "Blessed be the God and Father of our Lord Jesus Christ, the Father of mercies and God of all comfort, who comforts us in all our affliction, so that we may be able to comfort those who are in any affliction, with the comfort with which we ourselves are comforted by God" (2 Cor 1:3–4).

In the movie *Hunger Games: Catching Fire*, Katniss Everdeen is a teenager who is forced to fight against other young people for the entertainment of the elite. While she is preparing to leave for the arena, her coach tells her to "remember who the real enemy is." In the context of the movie, of course, he meant that the other contestants in the Hunger Games are not the enemy; the people forcing them to fight are. This is true in real life, too. We need to remember that the people we may fight with are not the real enemy. Satan wishes for us to be distracted by our pain and to continue a cycle of harm, but he is the real enemy. The people around us are victims of sin and pain, just like we are.

Breathe

If you need more time, try to distance yourself from people or situations that make you want to lash out. Avoid situations where you are tempted (Prov 4:14–15). It may take time before you can maturely handle a situation, so it is okay if you need to remove yourself so that you do not say or do something you regret. "Don't sin by letting anger control you. Think about it overnight and remain silent" (Ps 4:4 NLT). Jesus rested and meditated alone often (Mark 1:35; 6:46; Luke 6:12; 9:18, 28). Ecclesiastes 3:7 says there is a time to be silent and a time to speak. Sometimes, we must rest and meditate in the silence so that we can respond wisely.

When You Are Able, Talk It Out

We have talked about how some people think that turning the other cheek means that we must suffer silently, but as Ecclesiastes says, there also is a time to speak. Don't let things boil up inside you until they explode out. We may have to address issues for our own sanity, and we may have to address issues for the other person's soul. We should not allow others to behave sinfully, even if it is toward us.

- "If your brother sins, rebuke him, and if he repents, forgive him" (Luke 17:3 ESV).
- "Brothers, if anyone is caught in any transgression, you who are spiritual should restore him in a spirit of gentleness. Keep watch on yourself, lest you too be tempted" (Gal 6:1).

While the following passage is about church discipline, the principle of addressing wrongdoing with love and humility still applies: "If your brother sins against you, go and tell him his fault, between you and him alone" (Matt 18:15).

When we care about those around us, we can address issues with them in a way that shows love rather than selfishness. Correcting someone in love is very different from retaliation.

CONCLUSION

You can have compassion on people who are unkind without exposing yourself to additional harm. Displaying grace and mercy is in itself a show of strength. I've heard it said that mercy is having the ability to hurt someone but choosing not to exert that power. When we do that, a beautiful thing can happen. It can be refreshing and disarming for the person who is in pain. As Disney's *Frozen* puts it: "People make bad choices when they're mad or scared or stressed, but throw a little love their way and you'll bring out their best."

Every human being has felt tired, stressed, unloved, or empty. It is our job to recognize those feelings when they occur within ourselves and tap into God's never-ending love to recharge. Only then can we truly share the peace we find in God with others who display their own pain toward us. We want to be an example of peace and compassion to those who are struggling, not escalate whatever pain they are feeling by retaliating toward them. Colossians 4:5–6 says, "Be wise in the way you act toward outsiders; make the most of every opportunity. Let your conversation be always full of grace, seasoned with salt, so that you may know how to answer everyone" (NIV).

For Further Reflection and Discussion

1. How can we overcome our instincts of selfishness and retaliation?
2. How do the modern forms of retaliation mentioned in this chapter (clapping back, canceling, throwing shade, etc.) relate to the physical retaliation Jesus was addressing? What makes these behaviors equally harmful?
3. How do we recognize when we are operating out of defensiveness instead of love?
4. Think of a recent conflict in your life. How might applying the 'get curious about why others are acting this way' approach have changed the outcome?
5. Hurt people hurt people. Do you have any spiritual wounds that need healing, which influence the way you interact with others?

Outrageous Challenge

When you feel anger bubbling up, try square breathing.

Breathe in for four seconds. Hold that breath for four seconds. Breathe out for four seconds. Hold that for four seconds. Use those sixteen seconds to put away self-centered thoughts and reflect on what Jesus would have you do and say.

Write It on Your Heart

Meditate, memorize, or write the following verses:

- Matthew 27:12–14
- Luke 22:50-51
- Romans 12:19–21
- 1 Corinthians 13:1
- 1 Corinthians 13:7
- Ephesians 6:12
- Philippians 2:3–4

CHAPTER 2
GO THE SECOND MILE

MATTHEW 5:41

MACEY RICHARDSON

STEPPING INTO THE CHALLENGE

And if anyone forces you to go one mile, go with him two miles. (Matt 5:41 ESV)

"We are to be stars, ever pouring our light on the vault of night; flowers, shedding fragrance, though on the desert air; fountains, though we rise in the lonely places of the world, where only the wild things of nature come to drink. Always giving love and help to this thankless and needy world."[1]

WHEN WAS the last time you were asked to do something unfair? What about the last time you were *told* to do something unfair? How did you react in that circumstance? Did you get upset? Did you do the unfair thing? Did you have a choice?

This is a situation that almost everyone can relate to on some level, including the Jews of Jesus's time. Under Roman rule, the Jews had little say in how the government was run, the laws imposed on them, or the taxes they were forced to pay. Nearly every aspect of their lives was at the mercy of Rome. While they were generally allowed to go about their day working and worshiping as they chose, those freedoms were granted at Rome's discretion, meaning at any moment, for any reason, those freedoms could be revoked. One example of this was the law of impressment, which allowed a Roman soldier to compel any subject over the age of 12 to carry his pack for up to a mile. This was no easy task. The pack of a Roman soldier often weighed 100 pounds or more.[2]

So, imagine you are a Jew living under Roman rule. You often have the illusion of freedom, but the ever-present reality is that Rome is in control, and some take pleasure in reminding you of it. One such person is the Roman soldier who is stationed in your town. He takes every opportunity to exercise his authority over you and your people. On one particular occasion, he stops you on your way home from an exhausting day of work. "You. Grab my bag and come with me." You know pleading your case is useless; it will only make things worse. So you do what you're told: You pick up his pack and start walking. As you stumble along behind the soldier, struggling beneath the weight of his pack to keep up with his unburdened stride, going the wrong direction from your house, the only distraction you have is your own thoughts. So you think … less than kind … thoughts. About the soldier who uses his authority to bring you down. About the government that made it possible for him to do so. About everyone you pass who knows how unfair your situation is, but doesn't do anything about it. And who can blame you? This is a blatant injustice. It's how anyone would expect you to react, right?

Not Jesus. He offers a radically different perspective in the Sermon on the Mount, speaking to the very people who had to (literally) carry the weight of Rome's oppression. It is to them He spoke the words found in Matthew 5:41: "If anyone forces you to go one mile, go with him two miles." Wait—wasn't this supposed to be the Messiah, Israel's deliverer? The one who would free the Jews from exactly this type of subjugation and restore the throne of David? And now He's telling the people He's supposed to free that they should do *more* than the law requires them to do to help the people persecuting them?

As outrageous as this idea would have seemed for the Roman subjects of Jesus's time, it is perhaps even more counter-cultural in today's world. We are surrounded by voices telling us to protect our peace, draw hard lines, and never give more than we owe. And there are times and places where those things are absolute necessities. But Jesus calls us to something further than fairness. He invites us into a life shaped not by entitlement, but by love. If we want to live that way, we have to begin with His example.

GOING DEEPER

God has always gone further than what justice requires. He delights in mercy, restores the undeserving, and pours out grace until our cups overflow. And that same nature is perfectly embodied in Jesus. In Jesus, we don't just see a teacher or prophet telling us how to live; we see the God of the second mile walking among us, showing us exactly what it looks like.

Following the Footsteps of Christ

When Jesus calls us to go the second mile for others, He's not issuing an abstract challenge. It's a map of the very path He walked: one of radical love, costly grace, and humble service. The second mile is the trail Jesus pioneered every day He was on this earth, and now He invites us to follow.

We see this in countless moments throughout the gospels. As a rabbi, it was Jesus's duty to teach His followers God's will and the teachings of Moses and the prophets. But He didn't stop there. He saw each person in the crowds who followed Him:

their spiritual struggles and physical needs, their souls. In Mark 8:1–9, a crowd of over 4,000 had been with Him in the wilderness for three days. He had already more than fulfilled His role by teaching them, but when He saw they were hungry and tired, He didn't simply tell them to be warm and filled; He performed a miracle to ensure their physical needs were taken care of, after taking care of their spiritual needs.

As a miracle-worker, Jesus didn't just heal the sick. In Luke 5:12–13, a man with leprosy, a disease that deemed him unclean under the Law, fell at Jesus's feet and begged for healing. Jesus could have spoken a word and made the man well, but instead, He reached out and touched him, something no one else would dare to do. By touching this man, Jesus not only healed him of his physical disease, but He also broke down a barrier only He could to restore the man's dignity and holiness. Time and time again, Jesus made the unclean clean, not only physically, but spiritually. Just a few verses later, in Luke 5:18–25, Jesus healed a paralyzed man. Before restoring his legs, however, He told the man, "Your sins are forgiven." With every act of healing, Jesus revealed the full measure of wholeness he came to provide.

Jesus didn't reserve His ministry for the righteous or respectable. In Luke 19, He sought out Zacchaeus, a tax collector despised and rejected by his own people. Despite the crowd's grumbles, Jesus looked up into the tree and said, "Zacchaeus … I must stay at your house today" (Luke 19:5). Jesus knew how going to Zacchaeus' house would be received by the religious people of the area. But He didn't wait for Zacchaeus to clean up his life first. He made the first move toward him with mercy, and that mercy transformed him.

For Jesus, no act of service was too small or beneath Him, and no person was undeserving. On the night of His betrayal, Jesus washed His disciples' feet, including the feet of Judas (John 13:1–17). He knew what was in Judas' heart in that moment, but He still chose to show him love through service. When Jesus was arrested, He healed the ear of the high priest's servant (Luke

22:49–51), an act of compassion extended towards someone who was helping to arrest Him. Jesus didn't only help the people He liked when it was convenient; He served everyone even in the most difficult moments of His life.

These aren't isolated, random acts of kindness. They are a consistent thread in the life of Jesus. He always walked further, He always gave more, even when it was costly. Everything Jesus did on this earth led Him closer to the cross. Jesus's second mile didn't involve carrying a soldier's pack; it meant bearing the weight of our sins. But He was willing to walk that path because of His love for us.

To follow Jesus means more than walking in His footsteps; it means sharing His mindset. It is to take on the posture of a servant, to bear the burdens of others, to love even when it is not reciprocated, to forgive before it is requested. It is the definition of discipleship. "Take up your cross and follow me" is not just a catchphrase. It's the reality of the second mile. But we can walk it knowing that Jesus not only walked it first, He walks it still with us.

Revealing God's Character

The radical mercy Jesus shows us isn't an isolated event. It's a revelation of who God has always been. When we go the second mile, we are not just mimicking Jesus's behavior; we are revealing and partaking in God's nature.

From the very beginning, God has gone above and beyond what fairness demands. He didn't create a merely functional world; He created one teeming with beauty, color, and life (Gen 1). He placed humanity not in a desert of survival but in a garden of delight. Even after humanity rebelled, God sought them out. In Genesis 3, after the beings He created in His image turned away from Him, He did not turn away from them in response; He sought them out to offer them reconciliation.

When God rescued the Israelites from Egypt, He didn't just

deliver them from slavery. He established a covenant with them. He fed them with manna. He led them through the wilderness with cloud and fire. He forgave their grumbling and blatant rebellions, and He brought them to a land of promise. He allowed His presence to hover in their midst. He gave them judges and kings and prophets and priests. When they fell, He restored them over and over and over again; not by waiting passively for repentance, but by actively pursuing them and inviting them to receive His grace.

God did not establish a covenant with the people of Israel because He wanted subjects to serve Him, but because He wanted to pour out His love on a people who loved Him and strove to live according to His will. God told His people in Jeremiah 31:3, "I have loved you with an everlasting love; therefore I have continued my faithfulness to you." God's faithfulness didn't depend on Israel's consistency (they were anything but); it rested in His unwavering love.

It is because of that love that we see the ultimate example of the second mile: God sending His only Son not just to save us, but to become the sacrifice for us. This is not a reluctant concession or a backup plan. It is the fulfillment of the love story God has been writing from the very beginning. Romans 5:8 says, "God shows his love for us in that while we were still sinners, Christ died for us." God didn't wait until we repented or until we reached a high enough level of righteousness. He made the first move. While we were still turning away from Him, He was preparing a way back.

And He didn't stop there. God doesn't just forgive us. He adopts us. Romans 8:15–17 says we are no longer slaves, but children, heirs of God and co-heirs with Christ. The prodigal is welcomed back as a son, not a servant. In the same way, God brings us into His household, gives us His Spirit, and promises an eternal inheritance. That is the second mile. That is the heart of God.

God's character requires absolute justice, but that never comes at the expense of love. As one author put it,

> Law would be the first mile, love the second mile. Love includes justice, but justice does not necessarily include love. Justice that is not 'love-lit,' for example, might let a freed prisoner go out and starve to death. Life based on law will always call for retribution; life based on love will always call for restoration.[3]

If God were only a God of justice, He could have wiped out humanity at the first sign of rebellion. When Adam and Eve sinned, He could have ended the story. When Israel broke their covenant, He could have walked away. When Christ was rejected and crucified, He could have responded with wrath. But instead, again and again, God chose to restore what was broken. He clothed Adam and Eve when they hid in fear. He renewed His covenant instead of abandoning it. He raised Jesus from the grave instead of letting death have the final word. God is just, but He is also loving, forgiving, merciful, and gracious. Because of that, He will never stop giving us a path back to Him. He will never stop pursuing us even as we choose to forsake Him. We can never stray too far from a God who is willing to go the second mile to reach us. And when we choose to walk that second mile ourselves, we are living like our Father.

So why go the second mile? Because Jesus did. Because God always has. Because in doing so, we discover His nature and reveal it to the world around us.

LIVING IT OUT

In Action

So, what does it look like to go the second mile in our everyday lives? It might not involve carrying a Roman soldier's pack, but it does mean carrying burdens that aren't technically ours to carry. It means extending patience when you've already been patient. It means choosing kindness when bitterness would feel so much more satisfying. It means offering forgiveness before it's asked for, and sometimes even when it never will be. It means giving more to the person who seems only to take, loving the person who seems always to have it out for you. The second mile is about living with the kind of grace that doesn't keep score, the kind of grace God extends to us over and over again.

Sometimes going the second mile is recognizable and tangible: staying late to help a coworker who's behind, holding your tongue in an argument, stepping into a messy situation no one else wants to deal with, or going out of your way to serve someone who doesn't "deserve" it. But it can be difficult to know how to walk the second mile in various situations. Here are some practical questions that might help you identify areas where you can go the second mile in your life:

- Who in my life needs help that I've been avoiding because it isn't "my responsibility"?
- Is there a task at home I tend to leave for someone else that I could start doing willingly and unprompted?
- What's one aspect of my life (job, relationship, etc.) where I've been doing just enough to get by, where I could choose to go further?
- Is there someone who has been showing contempt towards me to whom I can respond with Christ-like love?
- Am I in a position to extend grace to someone who might not have asked for it yet?

In Attitude

Walking the second mile is about more than just action. It's about intention. For a long time, I thought the second mile was a way to measure how far I should go for someone, and that, as a Christian, that measurement was simply farther for me than for the average person. Peter had a similar mindset in Matthew 18:21 when he asked Jesus the question, "How often will my brother sin against me, and I forgive him? As many as seven times?" Peter thought he was going the second mile by forgiving someone more than the customary three times many rabbis preached, but he was still keeping score and wanted recognition for how far he was willing to go.

When Jesus responded to Peter by saying he should extend forgiveness to his brother seventy times seven, He was emphasizing that Peter had the wrong mindset when it came to going beyond what is expected. You can go the second mile with resentment, pride, or the hope of being noticed, but that is not what Jesus is calling us to. He is calling us to walk the second mile as He did, with nothing but love towards the one whose load we are carrying, expecting nothing in return. That shift in mindset is the first step to walking the second mile, and it's not always an easy one.

When Jesus talks about going the second mile, He isn't just giving us a longer or harder to-do list than everyone else. He's inviting us into a transformed way of seeing the world, how He sees the world: through the eyes of grace. Without the right heart, second-mile actions can turn into bitterness or burnout. Second-mile living is about embodying the character of Christ in the ordinary rhythms of life. That might mean choosing to see interruptions as opportunities. It might mean surrendering your "right" to be offended. It might mean practicing generosity, not because someone earned it, but because God has been generous to you.

Going the second mile doesn't mean there aren't boundaries. It isn't the same as enabling abuse or staying silent in the face of injustice. Jesus called out hypocrisy and flipped tables when necessary. But more often, He chose to respond with unexpected compassion. It's not about letting people walk all over you; it's about choosing to walk with them farther than they expected, because love compels you to.

This kind of life requires more than endurance or willpower. It requires abiding in Christ. As Paul wrote in Galatians 2:20, "It is no longer I who live, but Christ who lives in me." We don't walk the second mile on our own strength; we find strength in being deeply rooted in the One who walked it first. When determining if you have the same mindset as Christ when it comes to walking the second mile, consider the following:

- Is my service fueled by love or by feelings of guilt, pride, or obligation?
- Am I doing well because I want to be seen and praised, or because I want to love like Jesus?
- Am I holding back kindness until others "deserve" it?
- When I give my time or energy, do I secretly expect something in return?
- Do I see people and situations the way that Jesus sees them?
- What keeps me from walking the second mile—fear, fatigue, bitterness, or something else?

To go the second mile is to choose to go beyond what is deserved and strive for what is divine. It's where we choose mercy beyond measure, love in addition to law. In doing so, we become mirrors of the God who always goes the extra mile for us. So instead of asking, "Why am I being forced to walk a hard mile?" Maybe we should ask, "Where is God inviting me to walk a second one willingly, generously, and with love?"

For Further Reflection and Discussion

1. In what specific ways has God gone beyond what fairness demands in your life? How does

understanding His second-mile love change your motivation for serving others?

2. How can you tell the difference between second-mile service fueled by love versus guilt, pride, or obligation?

3. When have you experienced burnout or bitterness from trying to serve others in your own strength? What does it practically look like to abide in Christ while serving someone difficult?

4. How does the call to go the second mile challenge our culture's emphasis on protecting boundaries and demanding fairness? Where is the line between going the second mile and enabling unhealthy behavior? What "rights" might God be calling you to surrender for the sake of love?

5. How might your willingness to go beyond what's expected serve as a testimony to God's grace?

Outrageous Challenge

Look for a specific opportunity to go the second mile, not because you have to, but because you want to reflect God's character. This might mean doing something that isn't your responsibility, extending patience and kindness to someone who is being difficult, or responding to criticism or unfairness with grace. Pay attention to your heart. Are you serving out of love or keeping score? Ask God to help you see people and situations through His eyes of grace.

Write It on Your Heart

Meditate, memorize, or write the following verses:

- Micah 6:8
- John 13:14–15

- 1 Corinthians 13:4–5
- Galatians 5:13–15
- Galatians 6:9
- Colossians 3:23–24
- Hebrews 12:2–3

CHAPTER 3
LOVE YOUR ENEMIES

MATTHEW 5:44; LUKE 6:27

SIDNEY HARMON

STEPPING INTO THE CHALLENGE

Love your enemies, do good to those who hate you, bless those who curse you, pray for those who mistreat you. (Luke 6:27–28 NIV)

IN 1965, visionary musical comedian Tom Lehrer released a song called "National Brotherhood Week." Lehrer's recorded introduction to the song includes a line that is, in my opinion, pure gold: "I'm sure that we all agree that we ought to love one another, and I know there are people out there who do not love their fellow human beings, and I *hate* people like that!" Later in the song, Lehrer remarks that hate is as "American as apple pie."[1]

He's not exactly wrong, is he? But hate isn't a "virtue" exclusive to Americans, either. Humans seem always to be forming in-groups and out-groups. We love to belong to an "us," but the existence of a beloved "us" too often creates a despised "them." This was a problem even in Jesus's time, and He tells us exactly what to do about it: Love *us*, but love *them* too.

GOING DEEPER

"Love your enemies, and pray for those who persecute you." This teaching comes from Matthew 5:44 and Luke 6:45. If you haven't read those passages in a while, I'd highly recommend you go back and reread the entire chapters now to see these teachings in context.

These verses are excerpts from the Sermon on the Mount. Jesus is doing this fun little teaching thing where He gives them a common saying and turns it around: "You have heard this, but I say *this*." It's all about being better and obeying the spirit of the law instead of just the letter. He's challenging His audience to do more and more (1 Thess 4:1).

In Matthew 5, Jesus is teaching the basics of how to be good. In verses 21 through 26, He urges us to be people who make things right rather than people who indulge our own emotions. Anger, He says, can be as wicked as murder. He urges His followers to choose reconciliation.

Jesus keeps going with this idea. In the next chapter, you'll study the teachings in Matthew 5:38–42, and we can't forget what a revolutionary concept that is. When someone hurts you, Jesus says, let them do it. If someone tries to take from you, you should give to them generously. We are expected to act kindly toward everyone, even people who don't seem to deserve it. We must be good, even toward those who aren't good to us.

But He doesn't stop there; no, Jesus is no quitter! He takes it even further. It's not enough *not* to do bad things. It's not enough not to be cruel, not to lash out in anger, or not to retaliate when you are wronged. You have to actively *do* good things. But even that isn't sufficient by itself. You have to really *mean* it. Being kind begrudgingly is not what we're going for. You have to be *enthusiastic* about achieving righteousness.

In short, loving your enemies is a three-step process: forgive and set down your anger, choose to do good instead of harm, and keep working at it until your heart is in it.

LIVING IT OUT

Loving Your Personal Enemies

When Jesus instructs an expert on the law to love God and love his neighbor, the man asks what seems like an obvious question: Who is my neighbor? (Luke 10:25–29). Honestly, it's not a bad question to start with. If we are instructed to love our enemies, maybe we should ask: Who is my enemy?

Have you been alive for more than 24 hours? If so, you have probably had the experience of being wronged by someone! Consider someone who has hurt you. Maybe it's a friend who ditched you, a teacher who embarrassed you, a family member who ruined Christmas, or a woman at church who made a hateful comment about you. There's your "enemy." How successful have you been at letting go of your negative feelings surrounding that person? You can't love them until you start treating them well, and you can't do that until you let go of the hurt and anger.

But how on earth do you do that? Luckily, Jesus tells us right there in our verse: "Love your enemies and pray for those who persecute you" (Matt 5:44).

Last year, I had a nasty friendship breakup. We shared a community, worked together on tons of projects, and spent a fair amount of time together over the course of nearly five years. But when I disagreed with her on something I saw as a minor issue, things got out of hand faster than I could blink. Before I knew it, she was sabotaging my projects, spreading lies about me to our mutual friends, sending hateful messages to me, and ignoring my every attempt to make things right.

Honestly, it took me a long time to feel any way about the situation besides furious and heartbroken. I can admit that I stewed in it for a while. It hurt to realize that she and I will probably never speak to each other again, much less recover our friendship. One thought that comforted me was that, while I can't undo the past, I can always choose to be better from now on. So I took a deep breath, steeled myself for this incredibly unpleasant task, and decided to try out Jesus's approach. I started praying for her.

At first, the best I could do was something along the lines of "God, please help that woman to see sense and stop being such a selfish jerk!" (Obviously, this is paraphrased, but it's unfortunately not much of an exaggeration.) Most people don't realize that prayer, forgiveness, and compassion are skills that have to be trained like any other, but they are.

So I practiced my compassion. Just looking at the actions this person took, it was easy to write them off as unexplainable, unnecessary cruelty. It was easy to hate her if I didn't know why she was acting like that. But I didn't want to hate her anymore, so I tried to understand her. I thought about her all the time until I started to get it.

Why did my friend treat me like that? She was stressed and overwhelmed, embarrassed that she wasn't as perfect as she wanted to be, and defensive about it all. But most of all, she was just so, so lonely. She'd had so few real friends in her life that she didn't know what to do with my kindness. I was never going to be able to fix it, because every time I tried to help her, she thought I was trying to hurt her.

I had built this woman up into some sort of monster in my head—the person who ruined months of my life over petty drama!—but in reality, she was just a flawed, hurting human being. She never deserved my hate; she deserved my compassion. It took me months and months to see it, and even then, I felt like some sort of self-sacrificial saint for even trying.

And yet, when Stephen was being murdered (Acts 7:54–60), he didn't need 5–7 business days to turn on the setting for "attempting not to hate." He practiced ahead of time, so that when the moment came, he was able to say, "Lord, do not hold this sin against them."

When Jesus was dying on the cross (Luke 23:33–35), having been tortured and humiliated, His first thought wasn't revenge. His first thought was mercy: "Father, forgive them." I don't know if my forgiveness skills can ever achieve this level, but it sure is a lofty target to aim for.

Who are your personal enemies? Take this moment, right now, to consider. Is there someone you hate? Someone who hurt you so deeply that you aren't sure you can ever forgive them? Someone whose very existence leaves a bad taste in your mouth?

Pray for them right now. I'm serious. Right now. Ask God to surround them with good people who love them and treat them well, to help them with whatever they may be struggling with (for their own sake, not just to make them easier for you to deal with!), and to teach you how to love them. Talk to Him about your pain and frustration, and ask Him to guide you to a better understanding of the situation. Pray for healing and forgiveness for both of you. Try your best to mean it.

Loving Your Socio-Cultural Enemies

My congregation's Sunday morning adult class has been making our way through Genesis, one chapter at a time. A few months ago, we had a discussion that really stuck with me.

In the past, I've generally had the same few thoughts each time I read about Lot (Gen 13–14, 19). "Wow, what a loser!" was my first reaction, though it's not a particularly insightful or gracious one. Next: "What an idiot!" … Similar problem. I'm not sure if I ever made it past that second thought to reach anything more constructive.

This time, though, I stopped to really think about it. If you couldn't already tell, Lot has always kind of seemed like a bumbling, ungodly slimeball of a man to me. And yet, Peter, by divine inspiration, called Lot a "righteous man" (2 Pet 2:7)! I don't really want to argue with God on anything; He is always right. So if God Himself considered Lot a good man, it's worth asking why.

So, let's play our little empathy game. Let's look at Lot's story and ask why he might have done the things he did. If we can understand Lot, maybe we can learn to love him more like God does.

In Genesis 13, Abram and Lot recognized that it was time to part ways, and Abram gave Lot the first pick of the land. Lot saw that the land in one direction was beautiful, and he chose it for himself (maybe a little selfish, but perfectly understandable).

It just so happened that Lot's new land was the plains around Sodom, so Lot "pitched his tents near Sodom" (Gen 13:12). Time passed, and by chapter 14, Lot "was living in Sodom" (Gen 14:12). When we catch back up with Lot in chapter 19, Lot was "sitting in the gateway of the city" (Gen 19:1). This means he had probably worked himself into some sort of leadership role within the city.[2]

At this point, the main things we know about Sodom are that "the people of Sodom were wicked and were sinning greatly against the Lord" (Gen 13:13) and that God would eventually destroy the whole city (Gen 13:10). It was a nasty place full of awful people, and Lot wasn't exactly one of them (2 Pet 2:7–8).

Why, then, would Lot stay among these people, much less make himself a pillar of their community? Why would he stay among people whose very way of life distressed him, and why would he refuse to leave despite being warned of the city's impending destruction?

I think the answer is simple: Lot loved them. Lot moved into this city, got to know the people there, and once he understood them, he loved them. They became his people. Even though their wickedness broke his heart, he stayed with them, hoping that his example and his leadership could guide them to a better way of life. Lot loved those people so much that he wasn't willing to leave them to their suffering if there was the slightest chance of redemption.

As the story goes, God sent angels to warn Lot that Sodom would be destroyed for their wickedness. They told him over and over to leave, and he never seemed to understand the urgency of the situation. He kept hesitating every time.

It's easy for me, reading Lot's story from my cozy little armchair, to be frustrated at Lot for failing to just obey God already and give up on these hopeless people. I know that they are never going to listen. But to Lot, "Sodom" wasn't a historical shorthand for "irredeemable place." To Lot, Sodom was home. These people weren't storybook villains; they were his neighbors, his community. In that light, it makes a little more sense why he was willing to try anything and everything to save them from themselves. It's true that some of Lot's actions were incomprehensibly awful (see Gen 19:4–8), but even those choices came from a place of genuine care and compassion for people who seem not to have deserved it (see v. 10).

And yet, through all of this, God handled Lot with unwavering compassion and patience. God's messengers rescued Lot from his own well-meaning but foolish attempt to resolve the situation peacefully (Gen 19:10–11), warning him to escape the imminent destruction and to take his loved ones with him (v. 12–13, 15). When Lot and his family hesitated, God's messengers took them by the hand to lead them out safely. They escaped unharmed because "the Lord was merciful to them" (v. 16). I can't help but be awed by the tender and gentle understanding God shows toward this man who, honestly, is being a little bit frustrating.

It seems that God understood Lot and his actions and loved him despite his flaws.

The Old Testament doesn't really do a running commentary to tell us what to think about what we're reading. Usually, we have the story, and the interpretation is left up to us.[3] But as we've already discussed, when it comes to Lot's story, Peter gave us a nudge in the right direction. The takeaway is this: Lot was a good man who loved wicked people, and God loved him for it.

Lot is not condemned for the company he kept or for hesitating to obey. He is instead commended for his compassion.

One thing I've discovered over the years: A lot of people say they believe in treating everyone kindly, when what they really mean is they believe in treating good people kindly, and they've decided they're allowed to judge who is "good." Some of the fiercest Christians I've ever known fail at this final hurdle. It's all too easy to forget that God is the only one with the right to judge humanity and to dispense justice.

Unlike Lot with Sodom, the prophet Jonah had no personal relationship with the people of Nineveh. While Lot might reasonably have considered the Sodomites his enemies (see Gen 19:10), Jonah had no such right to personally hate the Ninevites; he had never even met them! And yet, he still saw them as enemies. He hated them so much that he wanted God to punish them and was angry with God for forgiving them (Jonah 4:1–2). Why? They were sinners. They were enemies of his culture.

You have heard it said: "Hate the sin, love the sinner." But if I might make a humble suggestion, I think that hating the sin shouldn't come first; loving the sinner should. Hating the sin turns you into Jonah, who is remembered as someone who fled from doing the right thing (Jonah 1:3) and tried to chastise God for being merciful to sinners (Jonah 4). Loving the sinner turns you into someone like Lot, who is remembered as a "righteous man" (2 Peter 2:7–8).

After all, Jesus is our ultimate example, and loving His enemies is kind of His whole thing. "God shows his love for us in that while we were still sinners, Christ died for us" (Romans 5:8 ESV).

For Further Reflection and Discussion

1. Which Bible stories might be good examples of how to love your **personal enemies**? Can you think of any bad examples?

2. Who were some of Jesus's personal enemies? How did Jesus act toward these people?
3. Who are your personal enemies? Why do you think they act the way they do? What can you do to improve your relationship with them?
4. Which Bible stories might be good examples of how to love your **social or cultural enemies**? Can you think of any bad examples?
5. Who would have been considered cultural enemies of Jewish men during Jesus's time? How did Jesus act toward these people? (Hint: John 4)
6. What groups of people might be considered enemies of your culture? How do you feel about those people? Do you love and feel compassion for undocumented immigrants? For the LGBT community? For Arab Muslims? For BLM protesters, abortion activists, politicians you don't agree with, or atheists?
7. Do you celebrate when "bad" people come to harm? Are you glad when good things happen to them?

Outrageous Challenge

Think of someone you consider a personal enemy or adversary, and try this: Have an intentional, friendly conversation (not an argument) with them. You might discuss a topic where you both share common interests, or you could ask questions about their family, work, or school. Pray for them before and after you talk.

Write It on Your Heart

Meditate, memorize, or write the following verses:

- Proverbs 10:12
- Proverbs 24:17

- Proverbs 25:21–22
- Romans 12:14
- Romans 13:8
- 1 Corinthians 16:14
- Ephesians 4:32

CHAPTER 4
BE PERFECT

MATTHEW 5:48

LANEY TRAVIS

STEPPING INTO THE CHALLENGE

WHEN YOU SEE or hear the word "perfect," what do you visualize? Please take a moment to think about this, then proceed.

Do you picture a sort of haven? The air is filled with the scent of honeysuckle, and golden sunlight sparkles in a clear creek. A light breeze brushes over a meadow as sweet peace fills the onlooker's soul.

Or do you remember a moment when everything aligned just the way you had planned and prayed? When everything seemed to be working in your favor?

Depending on what stage of life you are in, maybe you visualize your dream house. There are white walls with no crayon marks or scuffs, clean floors adorned with designer rugs, and fancy furniture with candles lit in every room.

Or do you see a person when you think of the word "perfect"? Her smile is bright. Her hair is thick and healthy. Her body curves perfectly, and her face is the very art of symmetry. She can do no wrong and is loved by all.

Maybe none of these things come to mind when you think of

perfection, but they are all proof that, from what I have seen, we tend to equate "perfect" with "flawless." Before we go any further, we must redefine our concept of the word "perfect."

When I was a little girl, I believed that I had to be flawless in order to be acceptable. I always had to smile in order to be considered good. I had to make good grades in order to feel any level of value. If I couldn't get something on the first try, I was a failure. If I expected ever to make God proud, I could never make a mistake. As a result of these lies, my life turned into a checklist.

This is the result of worldly perfectionism. This type of perfection focuses on external success and beauty, but the standard for this type of perfection is suffocating. It is impossible, ever-changing, and discouraging. Worldly perfection is the worst kind of all-or-nothing living because you're either on cloud nine or a failure. The truth is that worldly perfection is an unrealistic standard we will never be able to meet. Jesus knows we are incapable of being flawlessly perfect, especially in this realm of sin (Rom 3:23–25). So it seems as though we have actually been twisting the meaning of this word, when Jesus has defined it as something completely different and much less stress-inducing. A more reasonable definition for perfect is simply *something or someone being the best they possibly can be*, which we will elaborate on in the next section.

GOING DEEPER

Maturity

In the context of Matthew 5:48, the word "perfect" has the root meaning "mature" or "complete."[1] When we consider maturity, we think of reaching the most advanced stage or becoming fully developed. What that means for our lives is that human maturity is one's ability to handle emotions and situations as a spiritually-focused person, the best person we can be.

There are different areas in life where our maturity can be developed. Moral maturity is making good decisions that reflect wisdom and responsibility as a person who correctly distinguishes right from wrong. Beyond moral maturity, spiritual maturity includes realizing that there is more to Christianity than checking off all of the boxes. Disappointingly, we cannot simply do what is right and expect adherence to the "thou shalts" and "thou shalt nots" to set us up in the spiritually mature department. Rather, spiritual maturity requires actively pursuing a relationship with our heavenly Father and developing characteristics that reflect Him every day. Cultivating a deeper, more meaningful relationship with God is possible only if action is in step with knowledge, both growing together. Perfection here is not flawlessness, but an increasing connection to God.

Colossians 3:12–14 says,

> Put on then, as God's chosen ones, holy and beloved, compassionate hearts, kindness, humility, meekness, and patience, bearing with one another and, if one has a complaint against another, forgiving each other; as the Lord has forgiven you, so you also must forgive. And above all these put on love, which binds everything together in perfect harmony. (ESV)

Spiritual perfection is not found in checking off boxes but in every small and seemingly insignificant moment we choose God over self. The little choices grow us into the people we want to be.

Being spiritually mature is a choice, much like loving our enemies and choosing to clothe ourselves in each of the characteristics listed above. It is intentional. It is also a process; it isn't something you just wake up one morning and magically become.

Loving Our Enemies

Matthew 5:48 is embedded in Jesus's Sermon on the Mount. It is actually the last verse of chapter 5, and prior to it, Jesus gives an incredibly radical command on how to treat our enemies. Rather than harboring bitterness and hatred towards them, Jesus says we are to love them (Matt 5:44). I have always felt like this phrase is tossed around like free candy. The Bible class teacher's reminder to "love your enemies" is something that is so easy to say, yet so hard to do. This is frustrating because we treat it like being a Christian means loving our enemies will come naturally. Or worse, we act the part in front of our enemies, but once their backs are turned, we rip them to pieces with our harsh words and self-centered spirit.

I used to think that my enemy was someone who'd wronged me, someone who pursued problems as I fought to keep peace. I thought it would be clear that they were on an opposing team. But I have found that having an enemy is not that simple. An enemy can be anyone who cultivates opposition towards you, and this takes any number of forms, some more antagonistic than others.

Jesus intentionally tells us to love those who hate us because it is easy to love those who love us (Matt 5:46). It is when we choose to favor only those who love us that we choose to be no better than the world. We are kind and loving by human standards, through the world's influence. But in regard to our enemies, the world says to gossip, to slander, to judge, to turn a cold shoulder, to be a jerk, to do anything that could harm the character and feelings of our enemies. Jesus simply says we are to love them.

So what does any of that have to do with being perfect? Jesus says that loving our enemies makes us like our heavenly Father (Matt 5:45). Loving our enemies is just one out of many examples of lifestyle changes we are to make for God's glory rather than our own. Because let's be real—firing off insulting comments towards those we hate is much more self-satisfying than choosing to be kind to them. But being perfect, as our heavenly Father is perfect, means we choose to strive for excellence rather than participating in the ways of the world (2 Pet 1:3–11).

Humility

So spiritual maturity leads to fulfilling the command to be spiritually perfect in Matthew 5:48, and spiritual maturity is a life of action for Christ. One thing we have yet to mention is what it takes to be spiritually mature, and that is humility. If there is one thing you take away from this chapter, I hope it is this: In order to be perfect like our heavenly Father, we must embody humility as Christ did when He came down from heaven (Isa 53:2–3). A mentor of mine once said that humility is not thinking less of ourselves, but thinking of ourselves less. It does not matter how good we are or how kind we can be if we are not doing it for the right reasons, reasons that revolve around God and others.

Humility is what gets rid of the price tags (pride, hatred, etc.) and stamps "perfect" on our lives, because humble people don't measure their value by comparison to others. When we successfully grow in humility, it is no longer about us but about Him. We face choices as difficult as loving our enemies, walking away from partiality, and releasing the hatred that we have cultivated through gossip and self-righteousness. Our old way of dealing with these areas becomes increasingly disgusting and heavy on our hearts. Humility means we acknowledge the hard feelings, but choose to imitate Christ, because *it is not about us.*

Humility puts every good thing we are called to do in perspective. With it, what feels impossible becomes possible. Striving to be perfect like our heavenly Father takes self-denial and a whole lot of love. Humility is also not easy, because it is uncomfortable. Take time to ask for humility intentionally, but be prepared because He won't answer with a magic wand, but with real-life challenges.

———

I used to think love was something that would naturally expand within me, that it was much like this pleasant aroma simply floating about. I used to think humility was a form of self-hatred. I used to think that being perfect meant I was expected to have no flaws and to never fail. It's funny because being perfect in the eyes of God is the opposite of all of those false beliefs. Love has to be intentional (2 John 1:6), loving self is an essential step toward loving others (Matt 22:36–39), and mistakes are a significant part of being human (2 Cor 5:21). These are truths most of us will probably wrestle with for a while, but they challenge us in ways that will deepen our relationship with our heavenly Father.

LIVING IT OUT

So what do you think of when you see the word "perfect" now?

Do you see a Man? He sits among children. People are attentive to what He has to say. He is compassionate towards all, associating with outcasts and coming in contact with the unclean. He hangs on a cross. The nails that were beaten into His wrists prevent Him from breathing easily as He slowly dies. The blood and beatings hinder His sight. He is hardly recognizable, yet He never did anything wrong. He is flawlessly and completely perfect, but the problem is that we aren't. He died so we may be perfected in Him, complete and made whole.

The truth is that God has called His children to live a life that is higher than that of a checklist or any other approach to living for Him that is not in line with His Word. He has not called His children to be flawless, but rather morally and spiritually mature. He knows we are incapable of the flawless ideal the world has created. In allowing this truth to replace the lies, relief and freedom may be found. This is especially true for those of us who have grown up believing in the lie that we have to earn our salvation, and having this unspoken expectation hanging over our heads that we must constantly prove our worth. We place life-sucking expectations on ourselves that God never intended for us to experience.

Imitating the perfection of God is striving to be the best we possibly can be. It is choosing to not sit in the slop of our own impulses and desires. It is standing up and cleaning ourselves off for Him, even if it means we miss a couple of spots. It isn't about pointing out the mistakes we make or avoiding failure; it is the pursuit of being more like our Father in heaven. Rather than molding ourselves to our own concept of perfection, we are actually called to mold ourselves to Him.

With every new day, we are faced with the challenge to grow in our spiritual maturity by keeping the motivation behind every decision we make in check. We are challenged to strive for excellence for Him in how we speak to ourselves and how we look at ourselves in the mirror. We are challenged to be perfect as our heavenly Father is perfect, not as the world defines perfection. So take time to pray, take time to breathe, take time fully to know that God says you are of so much value (Matt 6:26). Take time to understand that because of this, you have everything you need to choose love in every moment and to pursue a humility that gives Him all of the glory in everything you do.

For Further Reflection and Discussion

1. What is your definition of perfect?
2. Have you ever felt pressure to be "perfect" as a woman, wife, mother, friend, or Christian? Think of a time when you were striving for perfection. How did it help or hinder you?

3. How does knowing the root meaning of "perfect" change the way you read Matthew 5:48?
4. How do we grow in humility? What changes will others notice if we become intentionally humble?
5. How do we imitate the perfection of God in our daily lives? Does this change as we mature?

Outrageous Challenge

Do one act of love that pushes you beyond comfort or habit:

- Show kindness to someone who is hard to love.
- Encourage someone without expecting anything in return.
- Choose patience or silence in a moment of tension.

Write It on Your Heart

Meditate, memorize, or write the following verses:

- 2 Samuel 22:31
- Psalm 18:30
- 2 Corinthians 12:9
- Philippians 3:12
- James 1:4
- 1 John 4:18

CHAPTER 5
TREASURES IN HEAVEN

MATTHEW 6:19–21, 24

HANNAH JARNAGIN

STEPPING INTO THE CHALLENGE

LET'S pretend for a minute that we are contestants on the popular, long-running game show *Family Feud* and the question is, "What is the number one indicator of success in American culture?" Top answers that would appear on the board likely include *fame*, *job title*, and *number of followers*. But "survey says" the number one answer would no doubt be … *money*.

To illustrate the importance our society puts on fortune, if we were to Google "most successful people today," we would see results like Elon Musk, Mark Zuckerberg, and Bill Gates—interestingly, all of whom also appear on the "wealthiest people today" list. Our cultural definition of success is intrinsically linked with and directly proportional to financial wealth and prosperity, and ideas like the "American Dream" and "the pursuit of happiness" almost always entail some level of materialism and affluence.

As a certified public accountant who deals with multi-million dollar financial statements daily, I know how big a deal the "bottom line" is to my clients and to our society. But God does not operate in our manmade systems. God does not necessarily care what our cash flow is. God is not impacted by our earthly wealth. He is King of an upside-down kingdom that stands in direct opposition to what makes sense to human nature and, even more specifically for us, what American culture values. So, as Christians, we might, and *should*, feel a tension between Jesus's teachings on money and our culture's opposite messages.

In the Sermon on the Mount, Jesus states that we cannot serve both God and money (Matt 6:24). He issues a very practical, but spiritually based, challenge early in this section:

> Do not store up for yourselves treasures on earth, where moths and vermin destroy, and where thieves break in and steal. But store up for yourselves treasures in heaven, where moths and vermin do not destroy, and where thieves do not break in and steal. (Matt 6:19–20 NIV)

Let's start by deconstructing the main subjects in this passage:

- **Treasures on Earth:** At the risk of sounding repetitive, earthly treasures are the societal things we place value in—a promotion at work, owning the biggest house on the street, having the most followers or the newest iPhone. What are we passionate about? What consumes our thinking? These things would be textbook examples of earthly treasures. These things are not innately wrong or bad. In fact, they can be blessings used for good. The issue is that we value them above lasting spiritual treasures. We run the risk of being distracted from what really matters and even consumed by their presence or importance.

- **Destroyers:** Jesus uses the depictions of moth and rust, which are very visible agents of destruction. We all know what moth-eaten sweaters look like and how damaging rusty nails can be. But there are other, hidden destroyers in the world: pride, anger, lust, etc. Essentially, any of those things we put price tags on (earthly treasures) can and will be destroyed by something—whether moth, rust, time, depreciation, or obsolescence. Nothing tangible that we can obtain on earth is eternal.

• **Treasures in Heaven:** Which brings us to heavenly wealth, which can never be destroyed. Now, that sounds great! Something we can keep forever? Sign me up! The problem is that these treasures are hard to define because they are intangible; they are spiritual in nature. If we knew exactly where we should be putting our value, wouldn't all Christians be collectors of heavenly wealth? When I think of "successful" people, by Christian standards, I think of those exuding the fruit of the Spirit, those actively living out their spiritual gifts, and those surrounded by and participating in Christian community with one another.

Jesus brings it home with a hard-hitter: "For where your treasure is, there your heart will be also" (Matt 6:21). Either our heart rests in earthly status, which will ultimately be destroyed, or our heart rests in eternity in the kingdom of God. We've already discussed putting value on treasure, but putting my *heart* on something makes it that much more serious. I hope I put my heart in the kingdom of God.

GOING DEEPER

One of the first lessons taught in a hermeneutics course is that when something in Scripture is repeated, it's extra important. The topic of money is all throughout Scripture. Including the Sermon on the Mount passage above, the Bible refers to money, wealth, and possessions over 2000 times.[1] So, what would a hermeneutics professor tell us to do when something is repeated over 2000 times? Underline, highlight, and draw an arrow to it in the margin—because it must be super important! In fact, it is said that money comes up in approximately fifteen percent of Jesus's teaching, including a large portion of His parables.[2] It is important to note, however, that in many cases, Jesus is simply referencing money to illustrate a point about the kingdom of God. In Matthew 6, we get both main topics—money and the kingdom—at once.

We cannot talk about the kingdom of God without also discussing Jesus's parable of the laborers in the vineyard, which gives us a beautiful picture of what this New Jerusalem (Rev 21:2) may look like. In this parable, the landowner goes out to hire workers first thing in the morning, promising a denarius for the day's work. A denarius was the standard daily wage for a laborer,[3] comparable to about sixty U.S. dollars today. Later in the morning, he hires more workers, again promising each a denarius. Midday, he again hires workers, promising the same pay. And one more time, about an hour before the end of the workday, he hires additional workers. At the end of the day, he pays all laborers the same wage—a denarius, as promised. Understandably, those hired early in the morning, who were working in the hot sun all day, thought they deserved more than those who worked for only one hour, even though the landowner paid exactly what he promised.

"But that's not fair," we say! This parable gives us a great picture of God's upside-down kingdom, which operates nothing like what we, in modern America, would call "fair" or "normal." But that is not what God promised; God promised goodness, generosity, grace, and forgiveness for all of those who call upon His name (Rom 10:13). If we are to be like Him, maybe that is what defines heavenly wealth: The more mercy, kindness, and love we offer those around us, the more spiritually wealthy we are. When we value those qualities and they become who we are, we will live differently from the culture around us.

Solomon discusses money and wealth numerous times in Proverbs. We can take Solomon's advice on the matter for two reasons: 1) He prayed to God for wisdom "to discern between good and evil" (1 Kgs 3:1–15). And God, pleased with this request, granted it to him. 2) Solomon was the wealthiest person of his time, so he had lots of first-hand knowledge about the desire for innumerable possessions and how to handle them. Solomon teaches us about prosperity with God (Prov 10:22), dishonesty or unrighteous wealth (Prov 10:2), and the value of wealth versus righteousness (Prov 11:4).

It's this last topic that is re-emphasized by Jesus in the Sermon on the Mount. In Ecclesiastes, Solomon says, "Those who love money will never have enough. How meaningless to think that wealth brings true happiness!" (Eccl 5:10). Earthly treasures are worthless. The value of the U.S. dollar comes from manmade government and changes constantly (have you seen the stock market recently?!). On top of that, we have no right to be self-righteous about our earthly success because even that is from God (Deut 8:18).

Paul also shares a lot of wisdom about money. One of his most famous—and misquoted—teachings on the matter is found in 1 Timothy 6:10, where he states, "The love of money is the root of all evil." I think the confusion in this passage comes from where the emphasis is placed. Initially, a lot of us read this with the emphasis on money: *Money* is evil. But that wasn't Paul's intention (in fact, in Ephesians 4:28, Paul encourages believers to work, earn money, and share with those in need). Paul's focus in 1 Timothy is on the *love* of money. This, again, is a heart matter, a foundational issue.

In 1 Corinthians 3:10–15, Paul teaches further about how important it is for believers to have a strong foundation in God rather than in the world:

By the grace God has given me, I laid a foundation as a wise builder, and someone else is building on it. But each one should build with care. For no one can lay any foundation other than the one already laid, which is Jesus Christ. If anyone builds on this foundation using gold, silver, costly stones, wood, hay, or straw, their work will be shown for what it is, because the Day will bring it to light. It will be revealed with fire, and the fire will test the quality of each person's work. If what has been built survives, the builder will receive a reward. If it is burned up, the builder will suffer loss but yet will be saved—even though only as one escaping through the flames.

Our heart, our foundation, our worth will be tested in order to reveal the quality of our treasure. A foundation of faith is paramount to getting the ultimate reward. So to answer our initial question of where our hearts and "wealth" rest, I have to say I hope my faith stands on a strong foundation, built with eternal gold and silver, as opposed to earthly wood or straw, which would be burned immediately by fire.

LIVING IT OUT

In a culture filled with social media influencers, Amazon two-day delivery, and the world in our pockets, how do we ensure our hearts are built on a strong foundation, with our ideas about wealth rooted in Jesus's teaching?

The risk with the heart is that we cannot always trust it. One of the most common misstatements in pop culture today is "just follow your heart." But our heart is deceptive (Prov 4:23); sometimes what we want, or what feels good, is not what will be counted as heavenly treasure in the end, so we have to trust God's word and His Spirit to direct our heart toward Him. God cares vastly more about our heart than our outward appearance (1 Sam 16:7). So the quality of our heart and where it lies are the ultimate measure of our worth.

Does this mean that we need to sell all of our earthly possessions, like Jesus advised the rich young ruler in Mark 10? When asked how the man could inherit eternal life, Jesus gave him one bit of wisdom, "You lack one thing: go, sell all that you have and give it to the poor, and you will have treasure in heaven; and come, follow me" (10:21). The man had so many things: riches galore! But he lacked something—he had so much treasure, but not THE treasure. After hearing this directly from Jesus, the man left sad because he did not want to part with his possessions. That is the crux of this passage: He valued his earthly possessions over any potential heavenly treasure, and he traded in eternal happiness for the temporary "here" and "now."

The rich young ruler's reaction to Jesus's command is in direct contrast to the disciples dropping everything to follow Jesus (Matt 4:20). That is what we are called to do; that is where true wealth and wisdom come from: valuing our relationship with the Father, Son, and Holy Spirit over anything this world has to offer.

Practically speaking, how do we invest in this "heavenly treasure" that will not be destroyed by moth and rust? Paul wrote to his friend and mentee Timothy regarding this exact question:

> Teach those who are rich in this world not to be proud and not to trust in their money, which is so unreliable. Their trust should be in God, who richly gives us all we need for our enjoyment. Tell them to use their money to do good. They should be rich in good works and generous to those in need, always being ready to share with others. By doing this they will be storing up their treasure as a good foundation for the future so that they may experience true life. (1 Tim 6:17–19, NLT)

So we see that the important thing is not whether we have money, but whether we use it as God desires. Paul redefines wealth for us by saying, "They should be rich in good works and generous to those in need." That is as simple as it gets. It covers every Christian, no matter their financial situation. In order to taste the New Jerusalem, experience true life, and enter heaven with Jesus, we have to realign our values and goals and redefine the Christian standard of "success."

For Further Reflection and Discussion

1. How would you define success? What things or values do you believe influence your definition of success?
2. Heavenly treasures include mercy, kindness, and the love we offer others. How does knowing these treasures are eternal change how you approach daily interactions? What's one specific way you could 'invest' in heavenly treasure this week?
3. Think about the contrast between the disciples who 'dropped everything' and the rich young ruler who 'left sad.' What earthly treasures do you find hardest to hold loosely? How might your life look different if you valued your relationship with God above these things?
4. Paul's focus in 1 Timothy 6:10 is on the *love* of money, not money itself. How do you recognize when your relationship with money or possessions has shifted from gratitude to love/obsession?
5. Can you share a personal experience where 'heavenly wealth' was used to advance God's work, in your life or someone else's?

Outrageous Challenge

Trade one earthly desire for something with a heavenly focus:

- Skip an online purchase and use the money (or time) to support a ministry or send a note of encouragement.
- Replace scrolling or shopping with reading scripture or journaling.

- When tempted to compare your life with others, pray for them instead.

Write It on Your Heart

Meditate, memorize, or write the following verses:

- Psalm 49:16–17
- Psalm 112:5
- Matthew 19:21
- Luke 12:33–34
- Colossians 3:1–2
- Hebrews 13:5

CHAPTER 6
DO NOT WORRY

MATTHEW 6:34

KAIT RICHARDSON

STEPPING INTO THE CHALLENGE

Worry does not empty tomorrow of its sorrow; it empties today of its strength. – Corrie ten Boom[1]

AS A CHRISTIAN who has been seeing a therapist for nine years and psychiatrists for eight years, has spent over a month (non-consecutively) as a patient inside three different mental hospitals, and has been diagnosed with three mental health conditions that all have some form of anxiety listed as a symptom, I really didn't want to write this chapter.

"Do not worry about tomorrow."

Some days it feels like that's all I do.

In today's society, five-year plans, vision boards, and manifesting a desired future are the rage. Let's be honest; this isn't just a modern issue—humans have always craved control. We search for any bit of control we can find, and we decide, *I know what I need and I know how to get it.*

We live in a world that has idolized the hustle and grind. T-shirts with slogans about forward momentum and planners with covers touting words like "You decide your future" line every shelf. Bestsellers have been written about controlling your destiny and working as hard as you can to get what you want. Being busy gives you bragging rights. Being tired makes you superior. We have competitions and petty arguments over who did more today, who's more tired, who got less sleep, and we feel anger and bitterness when someone outranks us in busyness.

Yet we can't seem to grasp in those moments why the hustle isn't getting us where we want to be. We don't understand which area we aren't trying hard enough in. What are we doing wrong? Why isn't this working?

We look to modify our plan, but not the destination. We decide to hustle harder. We play tug-of-war by digging in our feet on the side of success. We think failure is on the other side, the side we are at war with, and we pray it doesn't pull us into the mud.

But is it failure, or is it trust?

"If the devil can't make you sin, he'll make you busy."[2] If Satan can convince you to shift your focus onto the busyness of life, you won't have the strength or time to focus on your faith.

In his book *The Ruthless Elimination of Hurry,* John Mark Comer observes, "People are just too busy to live emotionally healthy and spiritually rich and vibrant lives."[3] It is impossible for your mind to successfully drive multiple trains on multiple tracks. You can do it; you just won't do it well or for long.

GOING DEEPER

I needed to research this topic because I couldn't grasp why God would command us not to be anxious. For myself, I know I don't *want* to be anxious, but I can't help it. It's an emotion, often leading to physical discomfort and angst that I would certainly do away with if I could. But some days, the divine answer to my pleas for peace from the glass ocean and iron butterflies in my gut is, "Take a Xanax and take a break."

A Greek lexicon is my go-to when a verse's message feels impossible or confusing. We often add nuances through misunderstandings passed down from other generations that cause the true message to be lost, so I like to go right back to the source and trust that the lexicon interprets the words more precisely.

In the case of Matthew 6:25–34, this seems to be what happened.

According to *A Greek-English Lexicon of the New Testament and Other Early Christian Literature*, the Greek for "worry" in this passage comes from a root word that means "a portion of a whole that has been divided," which is what sinful worry can feel like as it pulls our minds in different directions.[4]

This definition of worry describes what some call the "cognitive side" of anxiety. It is a thought process based upon your circumstances that, as described in the lexicon, pulls you apart and divides your attention between the present moment and the future, between trust and control.

This inner struggle is often rooted in a deeper mistrust, which often comes from fear or the feeling that the one you are being asked to trust won't hold you up as you need or want. But God offers us Himself, *in* perfect love and *as* perfect love, so how can a God like that make any decision that isn't for our ultimate good? As David Benner writes in *Surrender to Love*, "But being made in the image of God means that to fail to find freedom in surrender to God is inevitably to experience frustration and disappointment. No other love is worthy of our surrender. No other cause is big enough. Surrender to lesser gods will always become a source of bondage, not a spring of vitality."[5]

With knowledge of the Greek meaning and after hearing this quote from Benner, it is easy to see why Jesus commanded, "Do not worry about tomorrow." Because, as He says, "tomorrow will be anxious for itself. Sufficient for the day is its own trouble" (Matt 6:34 ESV).

Throughout the Sermon on the Mount, Jesus implores listeners to trust His Father, accept simplicity, and focus on

Kingdom things instead of earthly things. For us to handle today and exemplify the rest of Jesus's sermon in Matthew 5–7, from the Beatitudes to taking care of "the least of these," we must be in the present moment. We must focus on what we can and should do *now*, not what may go wrong tomorrow.

Jesus is known for offering rest to His followers, praying for their peace, meeting their emotional and physical needs, and quieting the storms in their lives. He does it for their struggles in the present moment. He doesn't promise the apostles He will quiet their storm tomorrow; He quiets it that day and tells them to have faith. He doesn't promise Jairus that his daughter will never be sick again; He brings her back to life that day and tells her to eat. Just as God gave the Israelites daily manna and commanded them to pick up only enough for the day and to trust in Him to provide manna for tomorrow, He commands us to trust that He has tomorrow in His hands and won't let us starve.

The bird and the flower trust God instinctively and know their lives are His to shape. Their destiny is His to decide.

Humans are a little trickier.

Why have we decided we know what we need more than God does? The One who created is also the One who knows. The One who knows is also the One who cares. And the One who cares always makes sure His children are cared for, even if it doesn't look the way they thought it would.

LIVING IT OUT

There are multiple ways this worry can manifest, not just through busyness and hustle. It can also look like worrying so much that you refuse to participate in God's plan.

If you're like me, the inner battle between acting and being still rages almost daily. I see injustice in the world—do I correct it or let God take care of it? I think often of Mordecai telling Esther that perhaps she was made "for such a time as this" (Esther

4:14), and then I think of David telling us to "be still before the Lord and wait patiently for him" (Psalm 37:7). So what do we do?

The first thing to do is to figure out where you are in the battle. Do you struggle with waiting, or do you struggle with acting? Are you someone who jumps in to take control and make yourself the solution without giving God's plan a chance? Are you someone who sits back and waits for the solution to come without offering your help in the process?

If you struggle with waiting on God:

- Why is this a challenge for you? Are you searching for control, are you falling short on trust, or is it a combination of the two?
- When you come to a crossroads, pause. Instead of jumping into action, say a prayer first. I like the Serenity Prayer: "God, grant me the serenity to accept the things I cannot change, the courage to change the things I can, and the wisdom to know the difference."
- Make a list, mentally or physically, of what you can control in this situation and what outcome you hope for.
- Say another prayer. God holds tomorrow, so be honest with Him about what you want to do, what you want Him to do, and what you hope will happen. He cares about your input.
- Do what you can and let God do the rest. Focus on today and only do the things you know you can control. Reference your list from earlier if you need to keep yourself on track. You've told God your thoughts, wants, and wishes; now let Him do what He knows is best for you, and accept the outcome—" If God brings you to it, He'll bring you through it."

To quote David Benner from the same book mentioned

earlier, *Surrender to Love*: "Far from being a sign of weakness, only surrender to something or someone bigger than us is sufficiently strong to free us from the prison of our egocentricity."[6] Surrendering is difficult for those who desire control and use constant action to create the illusion that they have it. Yet, when we are able to take a breath, pause, and look back to compare how our life has been when we've been in control versus when we've let God be in control, we know that God's way is the better way. Surrendering to God's perfect love for us frees us from the chains of ourselves, because we can see that we are perfectly loved, we stop fighting for control, and we know instead that we can trust the God who loves us. We can live in today instead of worrying about tomorrow.

If you struggle with playing your part in God's plan:

- Why is this a struggle for you? Are you scared of what others will do or say, are you worried you'll do the wrong thing, or is it a combination?
- When you come to a crossroads, pray. As mentioned earlier, the Serenity Prayer works here too: "God, grant me the serenity to accept the things I cannot change, the courage to change the things I can, and the wisdom to know the difference."
- Make a list, mentally or physically, of what you can control in this situation and what outcome you hope for. Even if you struggle with taking action, there is still an outcome you are hoping to see, so acknowledge that.
- Say another prayer. Yes, God holds tomorrow, knows what's best, and will bring His plan to fruition—but imagine the privilege of participating in that plan. In many stories in the Bible, we see hesitancy to act. Moses at the burning bush is a great example, making excuses and asking God to get someone else to free His people. God could have done that, but He chose

Moses and desired that Moses be part of the team that brought God's plan to the world, so Moses could become closer to God.

- Let God work through you. Look at the list of things you can control, because there is always an action you can take. I will never forget a preschool teacher telling me about seeing "suspicious bruises" on a baby and saying, "But I know God will take care of that baby." Yes, He will take care of that baby, but maybe He was trying to do so *through you*. Take the step to be part of God's plan.

When God provided the Israelites with daily manna, the Israelites had to gather the manna—God didn't just fill their bellies. A. W. Tozer says, "The driver on the highway is safe not when he reads the signs, but when he obeys them."[7] God has asked us to trust Him enough to move forward. If you're scared you'll mess it up, find some humor and comfort in this quote: "When God put a calling on your life, He already factored in your stupidity."[8] Humans never hit the mark every time, but God already knows that, and He's got it, and you, covered.

With all this in mind, we can see why Jesus says, "Do not worry about tomorrow." Not because tomorrow doesn't matter, but because God calls you to today, and He is already holding tomorrow.

No matter where you fall on the spectrum of the worry struggle, finding that balance between action and waiting is hard. And yet, if you're wrestling with it, that means you're trying, and God enjoys that, because He loves working alongside His people—especially when we mess up, because that gives us the precious opportunity to draw closer to Him. God tells a struggling Paul, "My grace is sufficient for you, for my power is made perfect in weakness," bringing Paul to respond as we all should: "I will boast all the more gladly of my weaknesses, so that the power of Christ may rest upon me" (2 Cor 12:9).

Escape from the trap of worry doesn't come from doing more or doing nothing, but from trusting the God who already holds the next day, and every day after that.

So let God hold you, mold you, and guide you. God's got tomorrow because He's got you. And God's got you because He's got tomorrow.

For Further Reflection and Discussion

1. Our culture has "idolized the hustle and grind," and "being busy gives you bragging rights." Can you think of specific examples from your own life or social media where you've seen this played out? How do you personally struggle with or resist the pressure to constantly be busy?

2. Thinking of a time when worry pulled your mind in different directions. How did it affect your ability to focus on the present moment and trust God?

3. Can you share a specific situation where surrendering control actually led to better outcomes than trying to manage everything yourself?

4. From the suggestions under "Living It Out," which has been the most successful for you? Which is the most challenging?

5. The chapter addresses both people who "jump in to take control" and those who "sit back and wait for solutions." Which tendency do you lean toward? What is one specific change you could make this week to better balance action with trust in God's timing?

Outrageous Challenge

When you find yourself distracted by worry this week, try this: Replace your worry with gratitude. Thank God for His care and provision, make a list of beautiful blessings in your life from God, or ground your thoughts in the present moment.

Write It on Your Heart

Meditate, memorize, or write the following verses:

- Joshua 1:0
- Psalm 55:22
- Psalm 94:19
- Proverbs 3:5-6
- Philippians 4:6–7
- 2 Timothy 1:7
- Hebrews 13:6
- 1 Peter 5:6–7

CHAPTER 7
DENY YOURSELF

MATTHEW 16:24; MARK 8:35; LUKE 9:23

MIRIAM GALLAGHER

STEPPING INTO THE CHALLENGE

HOW CAN I have a fulfilling life?

"Deny yourself" is not advice that we often hear. "Love yourself" is. "Take time for self-care" is. But "deny yourself"? Not very often.

To be sure, none of the other exhortations is intrinsically wrong, and, in particular circumstances, they may be the best exhortations to give. However, while they can encourage healthy practices, we must be aware that they can also encourage us to be complacent in sins like self-indulgence and self-obsession. Sometimes, we gravitate toward good sayings that don't actually challenge us personally (I certainly am guilty of this), and we avoid exhortations that demand something of us.

We live in a society that seems to view self-denial as a mental illness or an unfortunate lifestyle choice. Why would society value self-denial, though? It makes no sense to the world. The world values reputation, wealth, and self-actualization. But, in the Kingdom of God, the rules are very different.

"Then Jesus told his disciples, 'If anyone would come after me, let him deny himself and take up his cross and follow me'"

(Matt 16:24 ESV). Self-denial is foundational to what it means to be a Christian. But what does self-denial entail? If I deny myself, will I be ok? Or will I simply build up unaddressed appetites and end up hating God?

Many of us have grown up in the church. During our younger years, we may have experienced a great deal of legalism, whether in actual teaching or simply in our own perception of that teaching. We may have seen Christianity as a list of rules about what not to do, and we may have thought that if we did not keep the list perfectly, we would be condemned, thinking rule-keeping to be the self-denial of which Jesus spoke. As we grew, we may have discovered that God truly loves us and does not actually want us to be miserable. This is a beautiful thing. However, this experience may also have led us to be wary of self-denial because we think it smells of the lifeless legalism that we know is wrong.

And yet, Jesus says that it is in losing our lives that we will find them. Jesus's prescription is counterintuitive, but Jesus is trustworthy. And what Jesus is advocating is not legalism. Legalism, while an easy trap to fall into, is not Christian self-denial, because legalism is still about us, trying to attain righteousness by our own works, and telling everyone else that they ought to conform to what we are doing. Furthermore, legalism is not truly self-denial because it often does not actually involve denying the self. The self wants to feel better than others; it wants to tell them how to be. When the focus is on ourselves, we will become bitter about what we have undertaken or arrogant and judgmental toward others, or all of the above. At the end of the day, Christian self-denial is more demanding and more beautiful than legalism. So how do we authentically deny ourselves without simply becoming bitter and judgmental? We will not plumb the depths of this question, but we will explore various facets that will hopefully spark curiosity for further study.

GOING DEEPER

"For My Sake"

"For whoever would save his life will lose it, but whoever loses his life *for my sake* will find it" (Matt 16:25, emphasis mine).

The most important part of trying to deny oneself—and the only way to keep from becoming bitter—is to know why one is doing it. We do not deny ourselves for the sake of masochism. We do not deny ourselves for the sake of self-improvement. We deny ourselves for the sake of Christ. In his book on self-denial in the New Testament, Stuart T. Rochester notes, "The words 'for my sake' (literally 'on account of me') are important, as they indicate the christological focus of self-denying behavior, setting it apart from secular forms of self-renunciation and altruism."[1] This is where the primary difference between legalism and Christian self-denial shows itself. Self-denial is not rooted in following a list of restrictive rules. Self-denial is rooted in the adoration of Christ.

This is why the apostles could find joy in suffering. "Then they left the presence of the council, rejoicing that they were counted worthy to suffer dishonor for the name" (Acts 5:41). All suffering for the sake of Christ is the result of self-denial, because one must make the choice to deny self rather than to deny Christ to avoid suffering for His sake. Jesus blessed those who suffer for Him: "Blessed are you when others revile you and persecute you and utter all kinds of evil against you falsely on my account. Rejoice and be glad, for your reward is great in heaven, for so they persecuted the prophets who were before you" (Matt 5:11–12). It is a privilege to suffer—to deny ourselves—for Jesus's sake. He alone is worth it.

The Courts of Reputation

"How can you believe, when you receive glory from one another and do not seek the glory that comes from the only God?" (John 5:44).

What does it actually mean to deny ourselves? In his book, Rochester proposes one aspect of the answer to this question. He discusses the self-denial sayings of Jesus in the context of honor and shame and shows that Jesus draws a distinction between human and heavenly "courts of reputation." Both can bestow honor, and both can dole out shame. One of them, however, can bring greater honor. Therefore, self-denial involves a radical renunciation of earthly honor in favor of honor from God.[2] Rochester uses the story of the Good Samaritan (Luke 10:25–37) as an example of true self-denial. Jesus tells the story to a lawyer who wishes "to be seen as fully righteous" —or to "justify himself"—and "the disturbing message of the story is that he should deny himself. Love for God and neighbor demands a disregard for one's standing in the community, one's ritual purity, and one's personal safety."[3] Self-denial demands that we give up obsessing over what others think—even what other Christians think—in order to follow Christ. It demands that we be willing to bear scorn for the sake of love. "So Jesus also suffered outside the gate in order to sanctify the people through his own blood. Therefore let us go to him outside the camp and bear the reproach he endured" (Heb 13:12–13).

How to Find Yourself

But that is not the way you learned Christ!—assuming that you have heard about him and were taught in him, as the truth is in Jesus, *to put off your old self*, which belongs to your former manner of life and is corrupt through deceitful desires, and to be renewed in the spirit of your minds, and to put on the new self, created after the likeness of God in true righteousness and holiness. (Eph 4:20–24, emphasis mine)

C. S. Lewis ends his book *Mere Christianity* by explaining how to find yourself. You must deny yourself. Most of who we are without Christ can easily be explained by our upbringing or what kind of propaganda society is currently selling. It is only when we come to Christ that we truly become our own people.[4] Lewis writes, "How monotonously alike all the great tyrants and conquerors have been: how gloriously different are the saints."[5] It is only in Christ that we will find ourselves. But, as Lewis points out, if we come to Christ looking for ourselves, we won't succeed. We will find our life only if we aren't concerned about our life at all. We will find ourselves only if the one we are looking for is Christ.

> Submit to death, death of your ambitions and favourite wishes every day and death of your whole body in the end: submit with every fibre of your being, and you will find eternal life. Keep back nothing. Nothing that you have not given away will ever be really yours. Nothing in you that has not died will ever be raised from the dead. Look for yourself, and you will find in the long run only hatred, loneliness, despair, rage, ruin, and decay. But look for Christ and you will find Him, and with Him everything else thrown in.[6]

The Results

"Go, sell all that you have and give to the poor, and *you will have treasure in heaven*; and come, follow me" (Mark 10:21, emphasis mine).

"For this light momentary affliction is preparing for us an eternal weight of glory beyond all comparison" (2 Cor 4:17).

As we have hinted, self-denial is not supposed to be pursued for the sake of punishing ourselves. Nor is it to be practiced because God wants us to be miserable. No, God requires self-denial because He knows that it is only when we stop obsessing over ourselves and instead abandon ourselves to Christ that we can be free. And, in the end, there is a reward. We deny ourselves and rejoice in suffering because we know it will be worth it. Christ is worth it, and one day we will be able to see His face.

LIVING IT OUT

Now that we have discussed a little of what self-denial is, we will think about some practical ways that we can practice this foundational element of following Christ. Completely giving yourself to Christ is vitally important, but it can seem a little bit vague and difficult to imagine how that would look in the midst of our everyday lives, so we will explore a few concrete habits to implement. These practices are certainly not the totality of what it means to give oneself to God, and, as we discussed about legalism, they should not be seen as an end in themselves or a reason to feel proud of oneself. Nonetheless, they are good and important ways to practice self-denial.

Our small choices matter because they are practice for big choices, and rivers of small choices are what create the patterns of our lives. Thus, choices that seem like they don't matter can actually have an enormous impact. One small way to practice self-denial is to rejoice when we are required to serve. Thank God for the blessing He has given you by allowing you to serve, and ask Him to help you do it well. Then serve for Jesus's sake. Don't worry too much about whether you actually feel like rejoicing about it. This is something that I struggle with: I worry about my immediate emotional response and get trapped in thinking about it. The natural emotional response does say something about my heart, but how is God to change this response unless I do things that I don't want to do? We cannot become holy by waiting to want to be holy. We practice holiness. If love and service came naturally, why would there be so many commands to the early Christians to love and to serve? Self-denial is, by definition, saying "no" to ourselves. So, when we are called to serve and we really don't want to, let us not get caught up in trying to change our negative thoughts, nor let us act like martyrs. Rather, let us practice thanking God.

A second way that we can practice self-denial is by embracing the biblical discipline of fasting. The very essence of this discipline is denying ourselves something that we want. Now, one may ask, why should I fast? If the thing I would fast from isn't intrinsically wrong, why should I refrain from partaking in it? Well, apart from the simple fact that Christ seems to assume His followers will value this discipline ("And when you fast ..." [Matt 6:16; cf. 9:15]), fasting is an opportunity to practice saying no to ourselves. Justin McRoberts puts it this way:

> "Skipping meals can seem only loosely associated with the prac-tical, daily occurrences of life. But I have found that voluntarily and regularly removing a comfort from my life readies my heart to make more urgent, everyday sacrifices when they are called for."[7]

Practicing self-denial by abstaining from certain things doesn't need to look the same for everyone. For some, fasting from one meal may be a big sacrifice. Others may be able to fast for longer periods of time—one friend of mine fasted for seven days. Some people are medically unable to abstain from eating (however, there may be some of us who think that we are medically unable to fast when, in reality, we simply don't want to be hungry). This does not mean that there aren't viable options for these people. One can abstain from dessert, from coffee, from soda, from social media, from watching television, from listening to music ... and the list goes on and on. What one abstains from and for how long is less important than actually practicing this spiritual discipline from time to time.

The most potentially life-altering way that I will mention for practically denying ourselves is by deeply reflecting on the ways that we pursue status. Whose admiration are we pursuing— God's or man's? Rochester writes, "Those who renounce the quest for honor, welcome those of low status, and themselves become 'as children' find that this is the only way to enter the kingdom of God."[8] Has our quest for man's approval caused us to lose our wonder at the world because wonder is "undignified" and cynicism is "cooler"? Do we avoid certain people because we don't want other people to think we are weird by associating with them? Do we compromise personal convictions because we don't want to be seen as a killjoy? Do we seek glory from other people and not the glory that comes from God?

———

Many, many years ago, there was a rowdy young man who grew up with life handed to him on a silver platter. After he met Jesus, though, he decided to give it all away, and he began begging people for stones so that he could rebuild dilapidated church buildings, because he thought this was what God wanted him to do. He lived in abject poverty and fasted more than was healthy. He embraced lepers and cared for their wounds. He used whatever people gave him to bless other poor people. He preached to the birds, and he pulled worms out of the road so that they wouldn't be stepped on.

Many people today will no doubt question the asceticism— and, indeed, many of the actions generally—of Francis of Assisi. Francis does seem a little crazy, doesn't he? But Francis didn't do these things because he hated himself. He was motivated by love of God and man. Francis's self-denial was focused on Christ. Loving God and our neighbors is the point of our life here. Making sense to everyone around us is not the point. Being dignified is not the point. Enjoying ourselves is not the point. Love is the point. And love will sometimes make you do crazy things. That is why we would dare to deny ourselves—for the love of Christ.

For Further Reflection and Discussion

1. How can you distinguish between healthy spiritual discipline and legalistic rule-following in your own life?
2. How can you practice healthy self-care while still embracing Christ's call to deny yourself? Where is the line between self-care and self-indulgence?
3. What does authentic self-denial look like in action versus performative self-denial? How can you practice self-denial without drawing attention to yourself?
4. What messages from culture, social media, or your own inner voice contradict Jesus's call to self-denial? How do these lies make self-denial seem unappealing or even harmful?
5. What specific fears or concerns arise when you think about denying yourself something you want? How might these discomforts reveal areas where you're still clinging to control?

Outrageous Challenge

The act of fasting has become more of a diet trend than a spiritual practice in our society. This week, fast from something that you enjoy, whether that be meals, social media, or the best seat on the couch. Notice your attitude, motive, and train of thought throughout the week and reflect on how self-denial affects your spiritual walk.

Write It on Your Heart

Meditate, memorize, or write the following verses:

- 2 Corinthians 12:9
- Galatians 1:10
- Galatians 2:20
- Philippians 4:13
- Colossians 3:9–10
- James 4:10
- James 1:2

CHAPTER 8
FORGIVE 70 X 7

MATTHEW 18:21–22
KAYLA JENKINS

STEPPING INTO THE CHALLENGE

WHAT IS the thing you can't forgive? Pause. Think about it.

When you picked up this book and turned to this page to read this chapter, surely something came to mind. Every individual encounters situations requiring them to forgive others, as well as instances where they seek forgiveness themselves. Some of these situations are small, simple to forgive, like when your brother stole the last roll at dinner before you had a chance to get one. Others are more difficult, like a long-term struggle with your teenage daughter over her tone or her choice of friends. Still others seem impossible to deal with. Almost everyone has at least one impossible-to-forgive thing in their lives, and if you have not experienced this yet, then you probably will later. Manipulation, infidelity, assault, betrayal, rape, murder, and more exists in our world. There are times when sin rules our lives, and the consequences of sinful behaviors have a heavy hand in our interactions with other people. Big or small, sin causes some degree of suffering for those who commit it and those whom they commit it against. So, think about the sin in and around your own life and make this personal.

Sin is the source of all our suffering. Romans 5:12 says, "Through one man sin entered into the world, and death through sin, and so death spread to all men, because all sinned" (NASB95). This verse demonstrates the correlation between sin and every evil thing in the world, culminating in death. Sin leads to problems and suffering, and then leaves us to deal with it. When someone sins against us and it causes us pain, we will have a reaction to it. The real question is, what will that reaction be? Will we forgive? Why should we forgive? What does forgiveness even look like in practice?

If you are looking for a guide on how to forgive in ten effortless steps, then you have come to the wrong place. There are no easy paths to forgiving what we feel is unforgivable. For a year and a half, I have stumbled painfully through the process of redefining my concept of family after having mine shattered through the actions of other people. I have not fully made peace with what happened even now. The thing about life is that it keeps going, whether we have dealt with its events or not. Forgiveness is one of those concepts we could think about and struggle with for our whole lives without fully understanding. I am still wrestling with the idea of forgiveness myself, but we can wrestle with it together.

GOING DEEPER

The Secular View

Part of the confusion about forgiveness comes from the multitude of conflicting views concerning it. The secular world thinks about forgiveness differently from the general umbrella of Christian-minded people, who all think about it differently among themselves. Each denomination has its own subtle caveats on forgiveness. There are many wrong views because no one has a perfect concept of it. We will not get there either, but we can try to broaden our understanding.

As near as I can tell, the consensus of the secular world is to categorize forgiveness as a pleasantry. It is good for your mental health. In fact, most people would agree it is the best way to move forward after something terrible has happened—at least, they would agree when they are unaffected by the event requiring forgiveness. When it gets personal, though, when someone has caused pain or offense against me or my loved ones, it is entirely acceptable to hold a grudge. In the case of the "unforgivable things" we mentioned earlier, a grudge is even preferable. For example, there are not very many people in the world who expect a woman to forgive her rapist. The forgiving process, for the world, can also involve revenge. People who do not rely on God for perfect justice feel the need to exact their own version of it. We all have limits; it just becomes more obvious when we act without a limitless God.

The Religious View

For Christians, the problem with this approach is clear. When people view forgiveness as unnecessary and burdensome, they begin to attach strings that make it impossible to attain. Rather than being a soothing agent for the friction in relationships, forgiveness becomes a point of contention. Refusing to forgive creates another barrier that causes even more bitterness between people. The worldly approach tends to involve closing their hearts and futures off from the people who have hurt them to protect themselves from harm. They refuse to forgive because it would mean making themselves vulnerable to further disappointment and pain.

The view of the religious world is comparatively rigid when it comes to forgiveness as a requirement. From the beginning of their faith, many Christians learn that forgiveness is required of us and that it must be given abundantly. Forgiveness must occur regardless of the situation, and it must lead to a perfectly restored relationship at some point. After all, this is what it means to forgive as God forgives—right? How have so many come to this conclusion?

The Bible does exhort Christians to forgive as God does: "So, as those who have been chosen of God, ... bearing with one another, and forgiving each other, whoever has a complaint against anyone; just as the Lord forgave you, so also should you" (Col 3:12–13). As the people of God, people who have publicly become a part of His body, we are meant to function as He would act. This means we need to forgive as He would forgive. We find the teaching for God's method of forgiving our sins in 1 John 1: "If we confess our sins, He is faithful and righteous to forgive us our sins and to cleanse us from all unrighteousness" (1 John 1:9). Not only does God forgive our sins, but He also cleanses them. God uses the blood of His Son to wipe them away as if they never existed. After the dirt is cleared from our souls, our relationship with Him returns to a pure state. There is no purgatory, no waiting period. When we ask as His children, God's forgiveness is immediate and perfectly restorative. This is how our forgiveness must be, according to the regular interpretation.

We also learn about the consequences of refusing to forgive as God forgives. In Matthew 18:21–35, Jesus offers the parable of the unforgiving servant to Peter when he asks, "Lord, how often shall my brother sin against me and I forgive him?" (Matt 18:21). This parable points out the cruelty of refusing to forgive a small debt when someone greater took a larger one away from you. It highlights injustice and shows the lord in the story dealing strongly with the lack of forgiveness. At the close of the section, Jesus warns, "My heavenly Father will also do the same to you, if each of you does not forgive his brother from your heart" (Matt 18:35). This is a clear admonition. We must forgive. We must forgive as God does, which means perfectly and without reservation, or God will punish us severely. Earlier in the book, the sentiment appears, "But if you do not forgive others, then your Father will not forgive your transgressions" (Matt 6:15).

What could the problem be? If this is what the Bible says, then it must be true and right.

The Biblical View

However improbable it seems, viewing forgiveness in this way is both incomplete and damaging to our relationships with other people. When we expect forgiveness always to make things as if they never happened, and for others to offer it as immediately as we can force it, we are making forgiveness a burden that exacerbates the harm caused in the first place. God is a perfect and limitless God; it is no wonder He can forgive perfectly and immediately. We are not perfect beings, so our forgiveness takes time, patience, and effort, and will often remain imperfect. To pry the injured party's heart open by force and demand that everything go back to the way it was, "or else," will not make anything better. It is not a superior approach. It is not what God expects of us.

So, if this is not quite what God expects, what is? The case we have made above is a common mentality, and it seems solidly founded in the Bible, but there is more to consider. The mistake made in the understanding above is twofold. First, we have combined forgiveness and reconciliation into one big step. Second, we treat them with the same amount of necessity. God does command us to forgive without limit, as He does for us (Matt 6:15; 18:22), but this does not mean there are no lasting consequences from the harm that was done. In Luke 4:14–30, Jesus goes with His disciples to spread the gospel in His home-town, Nazareth. He brings the people He grew up with a message of good news out of love, but they respond with disbelief and violence. They take Jesus out of their town with the intention of stoning Him to death; as a result, Jesus leaves Nazareth and does not return in His lifetime. Since Jesus was a sinless and perfect man, we know He did not hold a grudge against these people. Even at the cross, He forgave those who put Him there (Luke 23:34). However, He did not put Himself back into harm's way by trying to reconcile with the town He knew would not accept His message. This example speaks volumes.

Not only did Jesus leave this example, but He also encouraged His followers to create distance when necessary. When Jesus gives His disciples the limited commission in Matthew 10, He makes stipulations on their behavior. He instructs them on what to bring with them, what to say, where to stay, and when to leave. "Whoever does not receive you, nor heed your words, as you go out of that house or that city, shake the dust off your feet" (Matt 10:14). Jesus did not advocate for hateful behavior, but He did encourage His disciples to know when they could not succeed and to put their efforts elsewhere.

Forgiveness is the God-prescribed method for dealing with pain induced by the sin of others who live around us. It is the best way to move forward in a godly way, and God requires it from us; however, forgiveness does not require us to return to the people who hurt and rejected us. The best way I have been able to think about forgiveness is as foregoing the right to expect payment or exact retribution for a wrong done against us. It is something I can do by myself, for myself, but this is the extent of what human forgiveness covers. Getting to this point does not automatically bring back the trust and familiarity of a prior relationship. The only thing forgiveness does is make it possible to get there again in the future.

Reconciliation

After we have been able to forgive, the reconciliation step of the process comes in. It is the part everyone is anxious to get to, and usually the part we want so that we can feel as though our wrongs have been forgiven. Everyone wants to get back to normal, but skipping this step is a bad idea, and it cannot always happen at all. In Romans 12:17–21, Paul gives the conclusion of a list of instructions promoting the unity of the body of Christ. In the verses prior to our section, he commands things like loving without hypocrisy, rejoicing and weeping with each other, and being of the same mind. Then, Paul gives instructions regarding retaliation. The Bible commands Christians strictly and in several different passages not to punish those who have wronged us. It is not our place or our business to punish someone who is not under our authority, something we struggle to learn from an early age. Everyone has seen or experienced an older child attempting to discipline the younger ones rather than allowing their parents to manage whatever situation arises. This is what we become when we attempt to retaliate against someone who has hurt us, and God forbids it. He does not, however, command us to have a conflict-free relationship with all men, no matter what.

Do not misunderstand, being at peace with all men is clearly encouraged in this passage (Rom 12:18). Be at peace, yes—but only if it is possible and only as much as we can control. God wants us to reconcile with each other, and He understands there are scenarios where this is difficult or impossible to accomplish fully. One example of this is infidelity in a marriage. While God hates divorce (Mal 2:16), He understands what infidelity does to a marriage, and He offers divorce in this one instance. Divorce does not mean we may not forgive; the injured spouse must still forgive as they have been forgiven by God. It would be preferable if the couple could work through their problems effectively, but Christianity does not force them into the same level of relationship as before. Another instance of this would be when someone who has harmed you dies. Forgiveness is still necessary, but reconciliation is obviously impossible on this side of heaven. There are a million other examples of reconciliation being difficult or impossible, which is why I propose that while God requires forgiveness, reconciliation is simply desired, not commanded.

An Example

I would like to offer this illustration, which makes the difference between forgiveness and reconciliation easier to recognize. Mental and emotional wounds are much like physical ones. They heal over time, but, depending on the severity of the wound, there are scars left behind, and some things never heal quite the same. If you get a paper cut on your finger, it stings but heals quickly. After a day or two, there is no pain and no mark; in fact, you could get a million paper cuts over the course of your life and only have a vague memory of being slightly uncomfortable. We receive paper cut injuries from people all the time, rude comments or similar frustrating behaviors. These are small hurts, quickly healed and forgotten.

We also experience more serious injuries, like if you fall on something and cut a gash in your leg, or if you break your arm. These things are more painful. They require time and care to heal properly, and they tend to leave scars; but in the end your body should work the same. These kinds of injuries to our relationships with others are also, unfortunately, common. These wounds can heal—everything can return to normal—if and only if the situation is dealt with appropriately. Catching someone in a lie is painful and destroys trust, but it is recoverable if addressed. These wounds need stitches and leave scars, but the relationship heals and functions just as before.

What happens when people lose limbs, though? Sometimes parts of our bodies are so infected, burned, or broken that the only option which will save the body is amputation. To refuse this treatment would mean agreeing to cause continual harm to the whole body until the wound destroys it. There are mental and emotional wounds we receive which require treatment with this level of severity. Some relationships are consistently harmful, and dealing with them as such does not imply a lack of forgiveness.

We must acknowledge the mental and emotional damage we

do to each other and properly care for it. If the physical wounds represent our mental and emotional anguish, then forgiveness is represented by the care we give the wounds. Forgiveness stops us from bleeding out and allows us to heal from the pain caused, but it cannot reattach limbs. There are many hurts that can heal and function just the same as before, if given the necessary time and care. There are also many hurts that will leave our lives and relationships permanently altered. They can recover, and they can function in a different way than before; however, trying to force our relationships to function the same way after suffering an amputation lacks realism. Setting new boundaries with a person who has hurt you does not mean you have forgiven less, or less effectively. Forgiveness requires mercy, love, and kindness toward the person who harmed us, but reconciliation requires us to treat ourselves with those qualities as well.

LIVING IT OUT

There are many things to hide behind when avoiding forgiveness, many things that hinder it. Ephesians 4:31 even provides us with a list: "bitterness and wrath and anger and clamor and slander … along with all malice." When these things are in our hearts, we can neither forgive nor reconcile. Instead of hanging onto our negative emotions, we should observe the very next verse: "Be kind to one another, tender-hearted, forgiving each other" (Eph 4:32). This is the heart God wants us to have, a heart which can say, "Father, forgive them; for they do not know what they are doing" (Luke 23:34).

I encourage everyone struggling with forgiveness to remember that God knows our hearts (1 Chr 28:9; Ps 44:21). He knows when we are serious about our attempts to forgive and reconcile. We will answer to Him and Him alone, not anyone else around us, for what lies in our hearts. Those who pressure and attempt to force forgiveness are not the ones we should be aiming to please. We should also keep in mind that, although

God does not demand reconciliation from us, He does desire His people to be unified. Forgiveness and reconciliation are not the same, but forgiveness should lead to reconciliation whenever possible.

For Further Reflection and Discussion

1. What specific aspects of forgiveness feel most "outrageous" to you personally—and why do you think that is? How does the world's approach to "cutting people off" or "protecting your peace" contrast with Jesus's approach to forgiveness?
2. What makes forgiveness so difficult to model well? How might our confusion between forgiveness and reconciliation contribute to unhealthy examples of both?
3. How does unforgiveness keep you emotionally tied to the person who hurt you? What "strings" do you tend to attach to forgiveness that makes it harder to give or receive? What would freedom from that look like?
4. How has the confusion between forgiveness and reconciliation created unrealistic expectations in your relationships? How might the pressure to "forgive and forget" or "get back to normal" actually prevent genuine healing?
5. How can we find peace in forgiveness if reconciliation is not possible?

Outrageous Challenge

When you find yourself struggling with forgiveness this week, try this: Meditate on the forgiveness God offers. Thank Him for His mercy and grace. Ask Him to help you extend the same love to others, especially when it seems impossible.

Write It on Your Heart

Meditate, memorize, or write the following verses:

- Psalm 103:10–14
- Proverbs 10:12
- Matthew 5:23–24
- Mark 11:25
- Luke 6:37
- Luke 17:3–4
- John 1:9
- 2 Corinthians 5:18
- Ephesians 4:32
- Hebrews 9:22

CONCLUSION

LET IT BE
AUTUMN RICHARDSON

IF YOU MADE it to the end of this book, you were guided by our authors through some of the most outrageous words ever spoken by Jesus. In each chapter, we confronted unsettling commands that challenge our assumptions and desires as well as actions that turn logic on its head. *Love your enemies. Forgive seventy times seven. Deny yourself.* The expectations are clearly stated, but the implications are costly and often misunderstood. So if you're reading this and wondering what comes next, the answer is not more effort. It is *surrender.*

Surrender is the thread woven through every outrageous word Jesus spoke. Surrender to God is not defeat. It is not weakness. It is not waving a white flag to signal giving *up.* Surrender to God is giving *over,* "relinquishment of the keys to the kingdom of self," which includes giving over your plans and outcomes to the One who holds the whole world in His hands.[1]

Here's the rub, though: The words of Jesus we've studied in this book are commands to obey. Surrender, however, is more than a command; it is a daily yielding that indicates trust. You can obey without surrender, but what "God desires is submission of our heart and will, not simply compliance in our behavior."[2] Surrender is an invitation. It costs us everything because surrender is more than adding Jesus to our to-do list. It's laying our plans and preferences at His feet and acknowledging that His will is better than ours, even when it disrupts and changes, and frustrates.

Mary offers us a beautiful example of surrender when she finds out she has been chosen to bear the Savior of the world as an unmarried, teenage girl. Talk about outrageous! This thing was happening. The angel doesn't ask; he tells her what is about to occur. She would have been obedient if she had simply assumed a passive compliance with the angel's announcement. But Mary says something that I find to be one of the most beautiful statements in all of Scripture. She replies in Luke 1:38, "Let it be to me according to your word" (ESV). These words are sometimes called Mary's *fiat* because of the Latin rendering of the phrase. *Fiat* means "let it be done."[3] What Mary is saying in that moment is that she is a willing vessel. She doesn't know the outcome or ramifications of what is about to happen, but she chooses to actively trust and give her life over to participate in the work of God. Mary's *fiat* begins Jesus's life.

Jesus then teaches us to pray a similar *fiat* in the Sermon on the Mount: "Your will be done" (Matt 6:10). Words of surrender and yielding. Words that He echoes to the Father in the garden as He is about to surrender to the unthinkable: "Not my will, but Yours, be done" (Luke 22:42). Jesus's *fiat* ends His life.

Surrender isn't only something that Jesus asks of us as His followers. It is something He modeled in His living and His dying. Surrender is the way of the cross. If that sounds too difficult, good. That means you're catching on.

Let your *fiat* be waking up each day and saying with your actions as well as your words: "God, I want what You want. Shape me, lead me, use me." Or in the words of Mary, "Let it be to me according to Your word." I pray that you discover over and over the blessing of placing your life in God's hands to gain a life that truly is upside down and outrageously good.

BONUS LESSONS

THE FIVE LESSON seeds below are designed to help classes or small study groups extend the conversation from *Outrageous* to a full 13-week quarter.

1. Leave Your Gift at the Altar and Be Reconciled

Text: Matthew 5:21–26

Jesus equates unresolved anger with murder, not because the outcomes are the same, but because both reveal a heart that is not right with God. Jesus tells us that reconciliation is essential and that we cannot worship God properly with that anger in our hearts.

Questions:

1. Why does Jesus elevate anger to the level of murder?

2. What does this passage teach us about urgency in peacemaking?

3. How can a church community create a culture of reconciliation?

Related Scriptures:

- Proverbs 14:29
- Proverbs 15:1
- Matthew 18:15–17
- 2 Corinthians 5:18–21
- Ephesians 4:26–32
- Colossians 3:13
- James 1:19–20

2. Take the Lesser Seat at the Table

Text: Luke 14:7–11

In a world that rewards success, status, and visibility, Jesus calls His followers to humility. His parable about choosing the lower seat reminds us that Kingdom greatness comes in the form of downward mobility.

Questions:

1. What external and internal motivations cause us to seek the "best seat" in today's culture?

2. How does Jesus' teaching challenge cultural ideas about success and leadership?

3. In what ways can we actively take the "lower place" in daily life and relationships?

Related Scriptures:

- Deuteronomy 8:2–3
- Proverbs 25:6–7
- Matthew 23:2–12
- 2 Corinthians 8:9
- Philippians 2:3–8

- James 4:6–10
- 1 Peter 5:5–6

3. Hate Your Father and Mother

Text: Luke 14:26–27

At first glance, this statement from Jesus seems not just counter-cultural, but offensive. But Jesus isn't calling us to literal hatred. Instead, He is asking for ultimate allegiance. Discipleship means putting Him before even our most cherished relationships.

Questions:

1. What does Jesus mean by "hate" in this context?

2. How do phrases that we often use in reference to our loved ones, such as "They are my everything" or "They have my whole heart" reveal ways we might unintentionally place others in a spot reserved for God? What does this look like with our actions?

3. What can we learn about the cost of discipleship from this passage?

Related Scriptures:

- Genesis 22:1–12
- Exodus 20:3
- Deuteronomy 6:5–6
- 1 Samuel 2:29–30
- Matthew 10:34–39
- Mark 3:33–35
- Philippians 3:7–8

4. Do Not Take an Oath

Text: Matthew 5:33–37

Jesus teaches that our integrity should be such that we do not need an oath to back up our word. As we speak, we should say what we mean and mean what we say. In a culture of misinformation, exaggeration, sarcasm, and spin, Jesus challenges us to purity through the words we speak.

Questions:

1. Why do people rely on oaths or dramatic language to prove sincerity?

2. What does a truthful life look like in a dishonest world?

3. How can believers cultivate speech that reflects God's character?

Related Scriptures:

- Leviticus 19:12
- Numbers 30:2
- Deuteronomy 23:21–23
- Psalm 15:1–4
- Proverbs 12:22
- Ecclesiastes 5:2–7
- James 5:12

5. Do Not Judge

Text: Matthew 7:1–6; Luke 6:37–42

Jesus doesn't say not to care or confront. He calls out the issue of hypocrisy. His vivid description of removing a log from our own eye calls us to humility, self-examination, and gentle restoration.

Questions:

1. What is the difference between judgment and account-ability?

2. How do we recognize and remove our own "logs"?

3. How can we practice Galatians 6 restoration in our churches?

Related Scriptures:

- Proverbs 21:2
- John 7:24
- Romans 2:1–4
- Romans 14:10–13
- 1 Corinthians 4:3–5
- Galatians 6:1–6
- James 4:11–12

NOTES

1. TURN THE OTHER CHEEK

1. "Bathos," *Encyclopædia Britannica*, 20 July 1998, https://www.britannica.com/art/bathos.
2. Brittany Kim and Ben Tertin, "What Jesus Meant by 'Turn the Other Cheek' in Matthew 5:39," *BibleProject*, 20 May 2024, https://bibleproject.com/articles/what-jesus-meant-turn-other-cheek-matthew-539/.
3. Tim Mackie and Jon Collins, "Jesus as the Ultimate Gift (Re-Release)," *BibleProject Podcast*, 21 October 2024, https://bibleproject.com/podcast/jesus-ultimate-gift-re-release.
4. Robert J. Hanlon, paraphrased and expanded in "Hanlon's Razor," *ModelThinkers*, https://modelthinkers.com/mental-model/hanlons-razor.

2. GO THE SECOND MILE

1. F. B. Meyer, *The Directory of the Devout Life: Meditations on the Sermon on the Mount* (New York: Fleming H. Revell, 1904), 115.
2. Cleland Boyd McAfee, *Studies in the Sermon on the Mount* (New York: Fleming H. Revell, 1910), 74.
3. Darrel Davis, "Go the Second Mile and Turn the Other Cheek," in *You Have Heard It Said ... But the Bible Says!*, ed. Bob McAnally (Lakeland, FL: Florida School of Preaching, 1996), 115.

3. LOVE YOUR ENEMIES

1. Tom Lehrer, "National Brotherhood Week," *That Was the Year That Was* (Reprise Records, 1965).
2. David Guzik, "Genesis 19:1," *Enduring Word Bible Commentary* (1996), https://enduringword.com/bible-commentary/genesis-19/.
3. I.e., in the text, there's not actually any moral judgment attached to Lot's wife's looking back. It just says what happened.

4. BE PERFECT

1. Frederick W. Danker et al., "τέλειος," in *Greek-English Lexicon of the New Testament and Other Early Christian Literature*, 3rd ed. (Chicago: University of Chicago Press, 2000), 995–96.

5. TREASURES IN HEAVEN

1. Andy Lee, "What Does the Bible Say about Money?," *Christianity.com*, 30 August 2023, https://www.christianity.com/wiki/bible/what-does-the-bible-say-about-money.html.
2. Jason Dulle, "Fact Check: Jesus Talked About Money More than Any Other Topic," *Thinkingtobelieve.com*, 22 August 2023, https://thinkingtobelieve.com/2023/08/22/fact-check-jesus-talked-about-money-more-than-any-other-topic/.
3. William D. Mounce, ed., "Denarius," *Mounce's Complete Expository Dictionary of Old and New Testament Words* (Grand Rapids: Zondervan, 2006), 168.

6. DO NOT WORRY

1. Corrie ten Boom, *Clippings from My Notebook* (Nashville: Thomas Nelson, 1982), 33.
2. Attributed to Corrie ten Boom in John Mark Comer, *The Ruthless Elimination of Hurry* (Colorado Springs, CO: WaterBrook, 2019), 20. Original source unknown.
3. Comer, *Ruthless Elimination*, 21.
4. William Arndt et al., "μερίς," in *A Greek-English Lexicon of the New Testament and Other Early Christian Literature* (Chicago: University of Chicago Press, 2000), 632.
5. David G. Benner, *Surrender to Love: Discovering the Heart of Christian Spirituality*, exp. ed. (Downers Grove, IL: InterVarsity Press, 2015), 59.
6. Benner, *Surrender*, 14.
7. A. W. Tozer, *That Incredible Christian: How Heaven's Children Live on Earth* (Chicago: Moody, 1964), 15.
8. Source unknown.

7. DENY YOURSELF

1. Stuart T. Rochester, *Self-Denial: A New Testament View* (Eugene, OR: Cascade, 2019), 5.
2. Rochester, *Self-Denial*, 20.
3. Rochester, *Self-Denial*, 24.
4. C. S. Lewis, *Mere Christianity* (New York: Macmillian, 1943), 190.
5. Lewis, *Mere Christianity*, 191.
6. Lewis, *Mere Christianity*, 191.
7. Justin McRoberts and Scott Erickson, *Prayer: Forty Days of Practice* (New York: WaterBrook, 2019), "Changing Toilet Paper."
8. Rochester, *Self-Denial*, 31.

CONCLUSION

1. David G. Benner, *Surrender to Love: Discovering the Heart of Christian Spirituality*, exp. ed. (Downers Grove, IL: InterVarsity Press, 2015), 58.
2. Benner, *Surrender*, 55.
3. Kierstin Richter, "What's Your Fiat?" *The Catholic Diocese of Shreveport*, September 2020, https://www.dioshpt.org/catholic-connection-magazine/whats-your-fiat.

CONTRIBUTORS

With a smile on her face and positivity in her back pocket, **Abby Foust** uses creativity in all she does. She graduated from Mars Hill Bible School in 2019 and received a bachelor's in medical humanities and psychology from Harding University in 2023. She's now finishing up her doctorate in occupational therapy from the University of Alabama at Birmingham. Hand-lettering, sourdough baking, and scrolling on Zillow are a few of Abby's current hobbies (although she might add a new one any minute!). With enthusiasm and spunk, Abby often says "yes" to more than she has time for, and she holds her friends and family dearly—cheering them on in all seasons of life.

A teacher at heart, **Jeanne Foust** taught high school students for nearly twenty-five years before taking on her current role of instructor of English at Heritage Christian University. She and her husband, Kevin, worship at Cross Point Church of Christ, where Kevin serves as an elder. Jeanne is profoundly proud of her two grown daughters, Hannah and Abby, and her son-in-law Braden, and is anticipating beginning a new role when her first grandchild is born later this year. Her superpowers include keeping her car (mostly) clean, devouring HGTV, and wrapping gifts.

There are at least three things that have deeply impacted **Miriam Gallagher**: she was homeschooled (you could probably tell if you met her), she is the oldest of six kids, and she was raised in a family that is serious about figuring out how to follow Jesus. A lover of languages, she is currently studying Spanish at Freed-Hardeman University, and she plans to continue studying Hebrew (with a splash of Greek and Latin) in graduate work. When she isn't doing schoolwork, she enjoys working for her Spanish professor, going on walks with friends or family, having deep conversations, and eating ice cream.

Sidney Harmon is an alumna of Freed-Hardeman University. After years of putting her Computer Science degree to good use by pursuing a career in software design, Sidney has recently returned to her Alma Mater, Mars Hill Bible School, to serve as its debate coach and resident technology geek. If asked to describe Sidney in one word, most people would go with "passionate." She is passionate about education, justice, politics, media literacy, digital citizenship, *Star Trek*, cats, and fighting every day to make the world a slightly kinder place.

A normal day with **Tonya Hayes** would include driving one of her three daughters somewhere, a cup of coffee with her husband, David, and reading a good book. Her family attends Petersville Church of Christ. She is also a member of the Shoals Community Band and a volunteer with the Kennedy Douglass Center.

Hannah Jarnagin graduated from Mars Hill Bible School and then Harding University, where she received a bachelor's degree in Accounting in 2019. She later went on to become a licensed CPA. She and her husband Braden live in Little Rock, Arkansas, with their cuddly Aussie doodle Shiloh. During her free time, she enjoys checking books off her to-be-read list, taking Shiloh on neighborhood walks, and hosting game nights with family and friends.

Kayla Jenkins is an amateur author with a love for the written word. She graduated from the Southwest School of Bible Studies located in Austin, Texas, in 2024. She is currently in the process of obtaining a bachelor's in biblical studies from Heritage Christian University and plans to use her education to bring glory to God.

Ava Johnson does not claim to be a writer but rekindled her interest in poetry and writing during a late-night bedtime battle with one of her toddlers. She is constantly surprised by the direction in which her life goes and is just happy to be here. Ava enjoys spending time with those who challenge her to be a better person, listening to podcasts, and traveling with her family: husband (Dustin) and their two-year-old twin boys (August and Arlo).

Melissa McFerrin is the Executive Assistant to the President and Coordinator of Women's Continuing Education at Heritage Christian University. She loves to read, travel, organize everything, and spend time with her husband, Clay; their new son, Levi; and their Christian family at the Chisholm Hills Church of Christ.

Autumn Richardson, M.Min., is the Director of Distance Learning, Coordinator of Radiant, and Instructor of Ministry at Heritage Christian University. She is currently pursuing a Doctor of Ministry from Portland Seminary. Autumn and her husband Adam worship with the Petersville Church of Christ in Florence, AL, where Adam is a minister. They have three adult children, a daughter-in-love, and three grandchildren who occupy a huge piece of their time and hearts.

Kait Richardson spent the better part of her schooling being "homeschooled," but "everywhere-schooled" would be more accurate. The Richardsons' love for traveling and creating memories is Kait's favorite part of her heritage. Now, her focus is on children, from fostering them in her home to working with children on the spectrum as a Registered Behavioral Technician. At her home congregation of Highland Park Church of Christ, she pours that passion into teaching the "littles" in Bible class. Children are her favorite mission, and creating memories with them is her favorite pastime. Next to kids, Dr. Pepper is her favorite thing, so if you see her in the wild, it wouldn't hurt to have one readily available.

Macey Richardson has a long history with Heritage Christian University, from sitting at her mom's desk in the Office of Distance Learning as a child to taking several dual-enrollment classes there during high school. Macey is a student at Freed-Hardeman University and plans to graduate in December of 2025 with a B.S. in Biblical Text and an A.A.S. in PTA. After graduating, she plans to pursue a career as a physical therapist assistant and find ways to use her Bible degree in her everyday life and at her local congregation. She loves hiking, coffee, and her cat, and she is a self-proclaimed expert in all things Star Wars and superheroes.

Laney Travis is a student at Heritage Christian University who will complete her A.A. in December of 2025. Though her future plans are unclear, she is enjoying growing in her relationship with and trust in God. He has blessed her immensely with opportunities and great relationships, and she looks forward to everything else He has in store!

After graduating from Mars Hill Bible School, **Tristin Wood** went on to get her bachelor's degree in special education from Freed-Hardeman University. She has been a special education teacher since. She now lives with her husband (Ben), daughter (Evelynn), and dog (Mike). She likes nature, crafting, video games, and drinking large cups of coffee.

CREDITS

RADIANT STUDY SERIES

The Radiant Study Series flows from a desire to provide quality biblical resources to Christian women. Written by women and for women, it features authors associated with Heritage Christian University. While somewhat patterned after the Berean Study Series, the Radiant series also includes extra material, such as prayer and journal prompts, Scripture-writing, and Bible-marking guides for each topic.

RADIANT

A CONTINUING EDUCATION PROGRAM   OF HERITAGE CHRISTIAN UNIVERSITY

our MISSION

Radiant exists for the purpose of cultivating spiritual formation within the hearts of women. By providing theologically rich resources, we equip women for study and scripture.

our VISION

Radiant women look to Him in all areas of life and are transformed into the image of Christ.

We offer

Classes online and on campus

Workshops and forums

Books, study resources, and content

Learn more at
www.hcu.edu/radiant
or scan the QR code.

Contact us!
Email: radiant@hcu.edu
Phone: 256-766-6610

ADDITIONAL RADIANT STUDY SERIES TITLES

Portraits of God's People (2024)

In Christ Alone: A Look at Blessings in Ephesians 1 (2023)

CYPRESS
PUBLICATIONS
An Imprint of Heritage Christian University Press

To see full catalog of Heritage Christian University Press and its
imprint Cypress Publications, visit
www.hcu.edu / publications

www.ingramcontent.com/pod-product-compliance
Lightning Source LLC
Chambersburg PA
CBHW031434120626
46545CB00006B/2408